MAKE A
STATEMENT

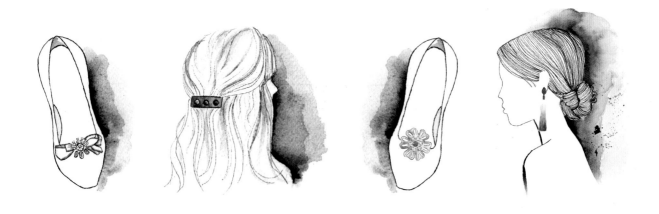

MAKE A
STATEMENT

25
HANDCRAFTED JEWELRY
& ACCESSORY PROJECTS

JANET CROWTHER & KATIE COVINGTON

CHRONICLE BOOKS
SAN FRANCISCO

Library of Congress Cataloging-in-Publication Data:
Covington, Katie.
  Make a statement / Katie Covington and Janet Crowther.
     pages cm
  Includes bibliographical references and index.
  ISBN 978-1-4521-3320-1 (alk. paper)
  1. Jewelry making. 2. Costume jewelry. 3. Fashion. I.
Crowther, Janet. II. Title.
  TT212.C675 2014
  745.594'2—dc23
                                    2014004103

Manufactured in China

Designed by Hillary Caudle

10 9 8 7 6 5 4 3 2 1

Chronicle Books LLC
680 Second Street
San Francisco, California 94107
www.chroniclebooks.com

Contents

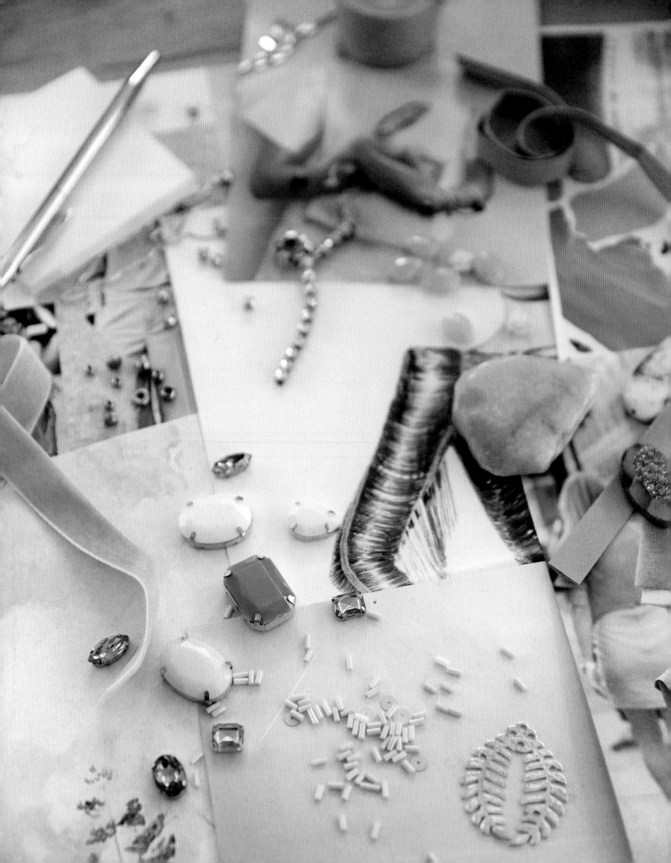

INTRODUCTION

We've been making our own jewelry for as long as we can remember. We started with macaroni necklaces, graduated to friendship bracelets, and eventually we moved to New York to design jewelry professionally for companies like Marc Jacobs and Anthropologie. We've always loved making pieces that nobody else has, and when asked where we bought our jewelry, we loved telling people that we actually made it. Around 2010, something changed. People started asking *how* we made the jewelry we were wearing instead of *where* we purchased it.

We started For the Makers to share everything we had learned from years of designing jewelry. For the Makers is an online destination that makes it easier to craft jewelry and accessories. We sell kits that include all the materials to make each of the projects featured on our website, and we stock our online shop with additional hard-to-find materials and supplies for designing your own projects. We search high and low for materials you can't find anywhere else, and when we can't find them, we have them made. We believe in making the things you own—treasured items you'll love and wear, now and for seasons to come.

People often tell us that they make our projects because it feels like a luxury to spend a few moments of their day creating something. They often send photos of how they've put their own twist on our designs to suit their style. Whenever a new For the Makers collection launches, we find that our makers can't get enough statement jewelry. When they finish a project, they're often surprised that their piece looks professional and chic yet was easy and fun to make. We wrote this book to share our favorite tips, tricks, and techniques from years of designing for some of your favorite brands, including For the Makers. With the right materials and a little DIY know-how from us, we think you'll learn just how easy it is to make your own personal statement jewelry.

Whether you've never picked up a pair of round-nose pliers, or you've been making your own jewelry for years, this book will have you creating and wearing your own statement jewelry in no time. Armed with the helpful information on the tools, components, and beads needed, you'll be ready to shop your local craft store like a pro. We'll then walk you through the basic jewelry techniques to give you the knowledge and confidence to dive into any of the projects included in this book. At the back, we've also included Sources and Resources, a list of our go-to shops, websites, and publications to make finding your favorite materials and make-worthy styles even easier.

Each of the twenty-five projects at the heart of this book makes a statement. And as a collection, the pieces range in style and complexity

from over-the-top necklaces embellished with crystals to elegant geometric hoop earrings. What these pieces do share is a style that feels elevated from the everyday, even when paired with something as simple as a white T-shirt. We chose projects that are updates of favorites from our jewelry boxes, as well as new pieces we were itching to design and wear. Some will only take a few minutes to complete (like the Studded Leather Band on page 64 and the Lost and Found Vintage Ring on page 84), while others might be weekend projects (like the Soft Statement Piece on page 123 and the Woven Collar on page 132). We hope you'll try them all!

As you make your way through the book, we encourage you to regard the projects as inspiration and feel free to inject your style and sensibilities into each piece you make. Playing with different materials, scale, and colors will allow you to come up with jewelry that's uniquely you. And remember, perfection isn't the goal. The inherent beauty in handmade jewelry resides in its uniqueness—it doesn't look like you picked it up at a store.

We hope as you read and craft these projects, you will trust your creativity, come up with even more ideas, and develop a love for handmade jewelry. Happy making!

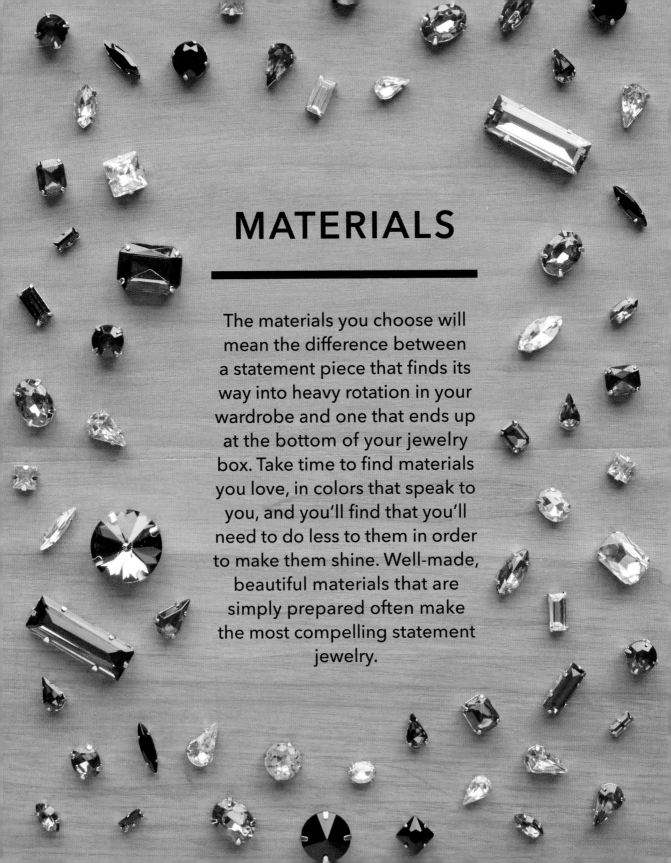

MATERIALS

The materials you choose will mean the difference between a statement piece that finds its way into heavy rotation in your wardrobe and one that ends up at the bottom of your jewelry box. Take time to find materials you love, in colors that speak to you, and you'll find that you'll need to do less to them in order to make them shine. Well-made, beautiful materials that are simply prepared often make the most compelling statement jewelry.

A WORD ON SOURCING

Sourcing jewelry materials can seem intimidating at first, but really, it's just like shopping for pretty things, so have fun with it. We often start by looking for items that excite us and sometimes end up creating a style inspired by our finds. Vintage shops, flea markets, and stone stores are helpful places to start. Online resources like eBay and Etsy make shopping for specific vintage components easier. Stores that sell ribbon, trims, hardware, and fabric are great places to get inspiration for using nontraditional materials in your jewelry.

When you're looking for the basic elements of a piece, it helps to familiarize yourself with the names of the various jewelry-making components, or findings. Findings are simply the components and materials used in making a piece of jewelry. This can mean anything from ear wires to clasps. They're the nuts and bolts that hold your statement jewelry together. Knowing their names will make it easier when you're talking to the people at your local bead store or shopping online. In this section, we included the technical names for components and beads so you'll be ready to shop. You will want to pay attention to the sizing and weight of the components you source, since you'll be wearing what you make. You'll find our favorite places to shop in the Sources and Resources section at the back of this book.

Bead shapes, from top left: barrel, bicone, briolette, bugle, chip, cube, disc, donut, faceted round, nugget, oval, rectangle, rondelle, round, seed, slab, tube.

BEADS

Beads are a perfect way to add color and sparkle to a statement piece. They can be strung, stitched, glued, or hung, and can be bought or made from an infinite number of materials. Beads can be found individually or by weight, but are most commonly sold by the strand. Bead strands are typically 16 to 18 in/40 to 45 cm long, but this can vary greatly, so use your best judgment when picking out strands for specific projects.

Bead Shapes

Beads are available in many shapes and sizes. They are available faceted or smooth. Faceted stones are sold with holes, as beads, or without holes, as flat-back stones. Smooth, polished stones are available as cabochons (with a flat base and convex top) or with holes, as beads. They're cut, polished, and sold alone or in strands. Some of the most common cuts you'll come across include briolette (teardrop shape), rondelle (donut shape), round, faceted round, seed bead, bugle bead (small tube), donut, chip, nugget, bicone (diamond shape), barrel, cube, tube, disc, slab, oval, and rectangle.

Bead Types

Here's a look at the types of beads you'll find used in the projects in this book:

CERAMIC BEADS come in a wide variety of sculptural shapes and textures and add an organic element to jewelry. The holes in premade ceramic beads tend to be too large, so we often make our own ceramic beads using polymer clay. This clay can easily be sculpted, baked in the oven, and painted to fit the particular style you're working in. For more on making your own polymer beads, see page 37.

GLASS BEADS are the most popular and varied type of bead. You'll find beads that are iridescent, opaque, translucent, or transparent. Machine-cut glass often looks just like natural gemstones when cut into faceted shapes and offers an affordable alternative to semiprecious stones. Tiny glass beads called seed beads are used for bead weaving, to create fringe, to embellish fabric, or in simple stranded styles. They come in vials, tubes, or hanks of several strands.

PLASTIC BEADS are an affordable alternative to glass beads. They are often more comfortable to wear, since plastic tends to weigh less than glass. Clear or swirled plastic resin beads can be extremely well made and you'll

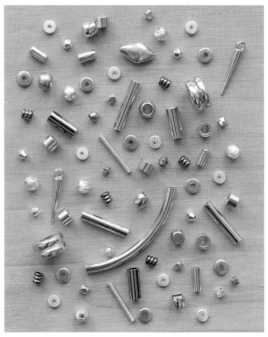

Bead types, from top: ceramic beads, glass beads, plastic beads.

Assorted metal beads including: tubes, rondelles, rounds.

see them used in chic, intriguing, modern pieces. Metal-plated plastic is a low-cost, low-weight alternative to metal beads. These beads are referred to as copper-coated beads (CCB), even if the final surface color is not copper. Look for plastic beads without obtrusive seams (left over from the molding process), and especially without flashing (excess material attached to the molded beads), which can catch on clothing.

METAL BEADS can be used as the main element in a piece of jewelry, as spacers between other elements, or as findings used in the construction of a style. They come in every metal and metal finish you can imagine, to match the particular chain or clasp you're using for a piece. Metal tubes, rondelles, and rounds are often used as bead spacers or in conjunction with headpins (short lengths of wire with a flat pad on one end used to attach beads to chain or other components).

Various rhinestone shapes including: round, emerald, oval, square, marquise, pear.

Semiprecious stones, clockwise from top left: amethyst, agate, hematite, lapis lazuli, pyrite, malachite, turquoise, quartz.

RHINESTONES add distinctive sparkle to statement jewelry. Made from glass, acrylic, or crystal glass, rhinestones are available with flat backs for gluing to surfaces, with pointed backs for placing in settings, and with holes for sewing to surfaces. For most of the projects in this book, we use pointed-back rhinestones that are already set in settings, so you can skip the step of finding a setting that is the right size and shape. You'll find rhinestones in many cuts, including round, emerald, oval, square, marquise, and pear. Rhinestones come in a slew of rich colors, including crystal, black diamond, jet, emerald, topaz, peridot, aquamarine, jonquil, and ruby.

SEMIPRECIOUS STONE BEADS are made from rocks, minerals, and gemstones mined from the earth. Amethyst, lapis lazuli, turquoise, agate, hematite, quartz, pyrite, and malachite are all types of semiprecious stones. Because of the variety of beautiful beads made from these stones and their gorgeous imperfections, they are some of our favorite materials to work with. But, for the same reasons, they're best purchased in person, rather than ordered online.

METAL COLORS AND FINISHES

Fine jewelry is made with precious metals like gold, silver, and platinum, while costume jewelry is made with base metals such as brass. Base metals are used on their own, or plated with a thin layer of precious metal. Most of the projects in this book use base metal, since it's more affordable and easy to find.

Precious Metals

If you'd like to upgrade to precious metal, try starting with the Geometric Hoops on page 53, a simple introduction to working with gold or silver.

GOLD chain and wire can be found in 10- to 24-karat varieties. The higher the karat, the more yellow the metal will appear. Here are some of the available gold options:

> **Gold-filled** wire and components, or findings, look like solid gold but are less expensive. They are made by permanently bonding a thin sheet of gold to a base metal like brass with heat and pressure.

> **Vermeil** also has the appearance of solid gold, as it's composed of a sterling silver base plated with gold. The gold plating is thicker on vermeil than on regular plating but thinner than gold-filled metal.

STERLING SILVER is a mix, or alloy, of silver and copper. It's widely available in findings, components, and wire. Sterling wire and sheet are easy to use for the Geometric Hoops (page 53) or the Hanging Pendant (page 112) projects.

Base Metals

For our purposes, a base metal is anything that isn't a precious metal, including copper, lead, nickel, steel, zinc, and alloys of these metals. While traces of lead and nickel are found in a lot of vintage jewelry, those base metals are not widely used today because of health concerns. If you are pregnant, please avoid sourcing vintage jewelry or components. Here are the base metals most commonly used in jewelry today:

> **Brass** is an alloy of copper and zinc. It resembles yellow gold and is available both plated and on its own. It's a great metal to work with because it's readily available, malleable, and heavy enough to feel substantial (read: expensive) when worn. Brass is a good material for any item that needs to bend or move, like a cuff bracelet, since it's flexible and won't break when bent.

> **Copper** is a reddish metal that is soft and malleable. It's often used as the base for plated jewelry components and findings, including wire. Copper easily tarnishes or oxidizes, so it's often seen covered in layers of gray, brown, or green.

Metal Finishes

Metal for jewelry components is also available in many finishes:

Shiny or high-polished metal is polished smooth and has a high luster.

Matte finish doesn't reflect as much light as a shiny finish and it appears flat.

Satin metal is somewhere in between a high polish and matte.

Antique finishes are made by applying a dark stain or wash over the plating and then selectively wiping it away. This finish is often found in American Southwest Indian jewelry, or vintage-inspired jewelry.

Platings

GOLD-PLATING comes in the same karat options (10 to 24 karats) as gold. Different sources carry wildly varying plating colors, so it's best to buy gold- and silver-plated components in person or from the same source.

SILVER-PLATING is a bright, light, cool color and can come in many finishes. Shiny silver plating tarnishes faster than other plating colors so it's often coated and sold as "tarnish free."

HEMATITE and **GUNMETAL** are terms often used interchangeably since they are both dark gray plating colors, although gunmetal tends to be a lighter gray (similar to steel) and hematite is darker (like the stone).

ROSE GOLD is a reddish pink gold that is often used for delicate styles or wire styles.

Plating colors, from top: gold shiny, gold matte, gold antique; silver shiny, silver matte, silver antique; gunmetal, rose gold, 10K gold.

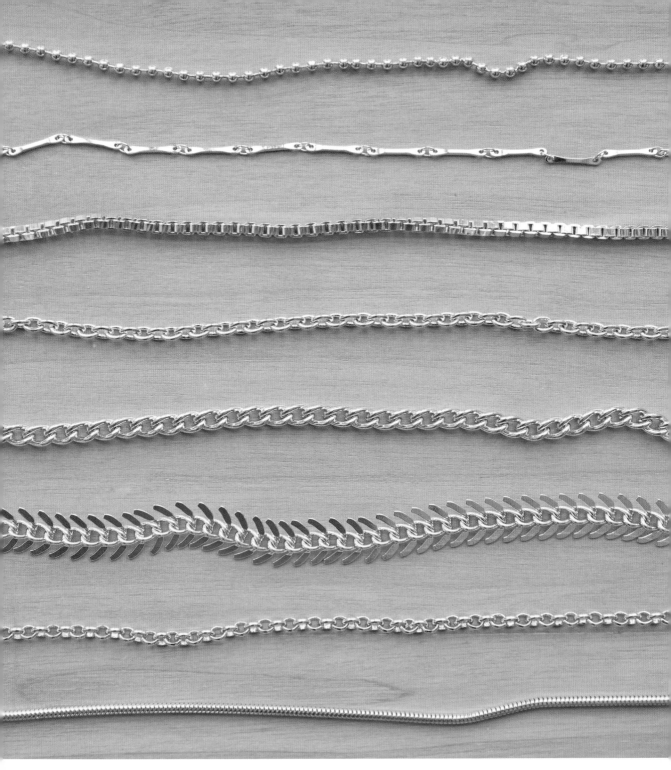

Chain types, from top: ball, bar and link, box, cable, curb, fishbone, rolo, snake.

Chain

Chain, a series of interlocking links, is a building block of statement jewelry styles, particularly necklaces and bracelets. Chain can be used as the focal point of a piece (as in the Vintage Rhinestone Chain Mix necklace on page 108), or as a base for hanging beads. Read on to learn about different chain types.

BALL CHAIN is formed from small balls of metal joined by small lengths of wire. It is essentially the same chain found in hardware stores and used by plumbers, although it can be found in smaller sizes made just for jewelry. We love to wrap it with thread.

BAR AND LINK CHAIN is made of bars connected with small links. It's most commonly used in delicate necklace styles.

BOX CHAIN is a series of interconnected flat, square links. Box chain is commonly used in bracelets and chunky necklace styles.

CABLE CHAIN is made of circular or oval links that are joined at right angles. It's the most common type of chain for delicate necklaces (like in the Multirow Amulet, page 101).

CURB CHAIN has links that interlock with each other when laid flat. It's available in a variety of widths and thicknesses. It's our go-to type of chain for short statement necklaces (like the Woven Collar on page 132 and Vintage Rhinestone Chain Mix on page 108). Curb chain can also be connected with two thin links rather than one larger one. This is referred to as **DOUBLE CURB CHAIN**.

FISHBONE CHAIN has the appearance of a fish bone, with a flat V-shape protruding from each link. Use the V-shapes to wrap with thread or thin ribbon or to add a touch of rebel to a chunky chain style.

ROLO CHAIN is very similar to cable chain, except the links are flat circles instead of round wire. It's a perfect chain to use when attaching charms and beads because of its large, open links.

SNAKE CHAIN is a very tightly linked chain, fluidly solid, that has a zigzag or snake look. Since it's so tightly linked, it must be connected to other elements with end caps (findings that conceal the unsightly ends of chain or trims) rather than jump rings (metal rings used to connect jewelry elements). It's most often used on its own or to connect elements (like in the High-Low Tie Back on page 98).

WIRE

Wire is a basic building block of jewelry design because it's used to connect elements. It's available in many metal finishes and a range of thicknesses. We tend to use round wire for beading, but square wire and half-round wire are also available.

Temper

Wire is sold in several tempers that determine how easily the wire can bend. Soft wire is the easiest to manipulate but the least durable when worn. One way to get around this is to work-harden the metal while you create your jewelry. Traditionally, metalsmiths use hammers to work-harden metal, but for small wire projects, the easiest way to work-harden metal is to gently open and close chain-nose pliers (see page 29) repeatedly over the entire length of the wire.

DEAD SOFT WIRE is the easiest to manipulate with pliers and ideal for wire-working.

FULL-HARD WIRE is very sturdy but difficult to work with.

HALF-HARD WIRE is somewhere between dead soft and full hard and is ideal for components that must retain their shape, like ear wires (a loop of wire that passes through the wearer's earlobe to fasten an earring in place) or jump rings.

Thickness

Wire is typically purchased by thickness, or gauge. In the United States and Canada, this thickness is referred to by the gauge, while in Europe it's often referred to by the millimeter. The higher the gauge is, the thinner the wire. Throughout the book we'll refer to wire sizes as small, medium, or large. Here are the relative sizes of the wires:

Thin wire: 24 to 28 gauge, or less than 0.6 mm

Medium wire: 18 to 22 gauge, or 0.7 to 1.2 mm

Large wire: more than 16 gauge, or 1.3 mm

Wire thickness, from top: large thickness, medium thickness, thin thickness.

JEWELRY FINDINGS AND COMPONENTS

Much of jewelry design and creation is engineering the piece to lie on your body in a natural, unobtrusive way, so take the time to be thoughtful about the findings you choose. Your effort will pay off with a well-designed piece that lasts for seasons to come.

Clasps

Every project deserves an elegant ending. A clasp aesthetically finishes a piece of jewelry while keeping it secure around your neck or wrist. The style of jewelry dictates the best type of clasp to use for each project. Here are the sizes of clasps:

Small clasps: less than 5 mm

Medium clasps: 6 to 15 mm

Large clasps: more than 15 mm

Various clasps, including: lobster, S-hook, toggle, spring ring.

LOBSTER CLASPS are popular choices in our studio. They use the same spring mechanism as a spring ring but with an elongated claw shape. They are used on necklaces and bracelets.

S-HOOKS are double-ended hook clasps, shaped like an S. Pinching the end of the S secures the clasp. Look for hooks made with a metal that is flexible, because these will wear best.

SPRING RINGS are great for delicate as well as casual styles. They are used with a closed jump ring to make a complete clasp. They contain a small spring, which automatically closes when released, making them popular for delicate chain styles.

TOGGLES are also called bar-and-ring clasps. One end of the clasp is a closed loop and the other end is a T-shaped bar. When clasped, the bar sits on top of the loop, securing it. Toggles are often used in bracelets, since they are easy to clasp with one hand.

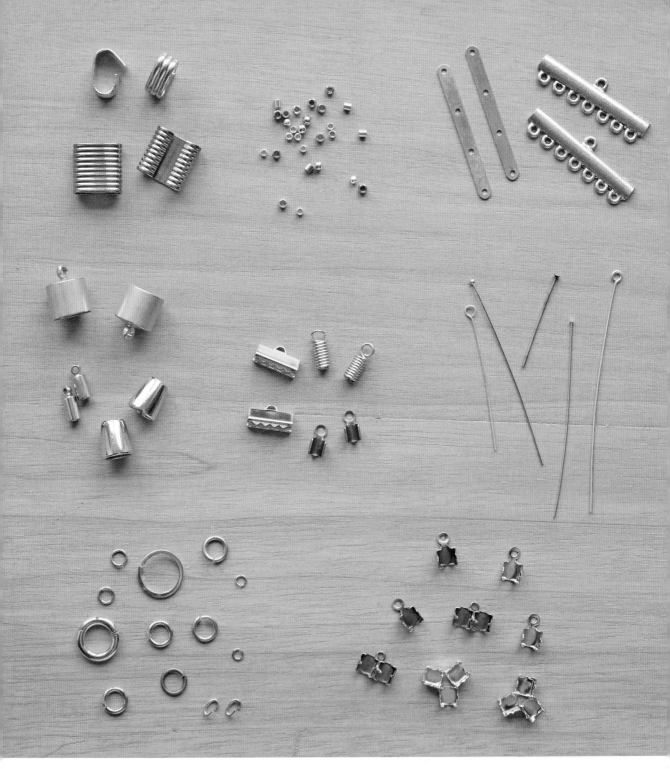

Ends and connectors, from top left: connectors; crimp beads; end bars; end caps; foldover crimps and coil ends; headpins, ball pins, and eye pins; jump rings; rhinestone chain ends.

Ends and Connectors

CONNECTOR is a general term for any component that connects two other components. Often these are riffs on jump rings, including flat wire ovals, figure-eight shapes, or two attached circles. In the Gold Bib on page 105, we use double-bar connectors with loops on each end to hold two rings at a specific distance to create a sleek grid.

CRIMP BEADS are used to secure beading wire to a clasp. They are soft, cylindrical tubes with large holes. When squeezed tightly with pliers, they hold the beading wire in place. These flattened connectors can then be covered with crimp covers for a decorative look. For step-by-step instructions on using crimp beads, see page 36.

END BARS are used to space out strands of multistrand necklaces or bracelets. They are available with as few as two, or more than a dozen loops. Some end bars also act as clasps.

END CAPS cover rope, beading wires, or other soft stringing materials. We often add a bit of glue to the bottom of the cap before we insert the stringing material, for extra durability. End caps come in different sizes and shapes: cylinders, cones, or coils.

FOLDOVER CRIMPS and **COIL ENDS** cover the ends of ribbon, cord, leather, or snake chain. Metal tabs are folded over the material, securing it inside. A clasp or jump ring can be added to the loop on the end of the crimp.

HEADPINS, BALL PINS, and **EYE PINS** are short lengths of wire used to attach beads to chain or other components. Headpins have a flat end to secure the bead, while ball pins have a small bead at the end of the wire. Eye pins have a small loop at the end of the wire used to attach multiple elements, like in a rosary. Bead looping and wire wrapping are fundamental techniques for creating beaded statement jewelry. When you're shopping for these findings, make sure the length and thickness of the pin works with the bead you're attaching. Check to make sure the head, eye, or pin diameter is larger than the hole in the bead, so that it keeps it from slipping off, and that there's enough room on the end for a loop. If you don't have an eye pin on hand, you can use wire to create a loop on each end.

JUMP RINGS are round or oval wire rings used to attach or connect one element (like a chain) to another element (like a clasp). They come in any thickness, diameter, or finish. Your jewelry is only as strong as the weakest jump ring you use, so make sure the ones you are using are relative in size and thickness to whatever you are connecting. Closed jump rings are soldered shut and are used for clasps and delicate connections. Throughout the book, we'll refer to jump ring sizes as small, medium, or large rings:

> **Small jump rings:** 2 to 5 mm
>
> **Medium jump rings:** 6 to 10 mm
>
> **Large jump rings:** more than 10 mm

RHINESTONE CHAIN ENDS are used to attach rhinestone chain to a clasp or jump ring. Place the last stone setting in the connector and press the prongs over the stone to secure it. When shopping for these components, look for connectors that are the same size as the rhinestone setting.

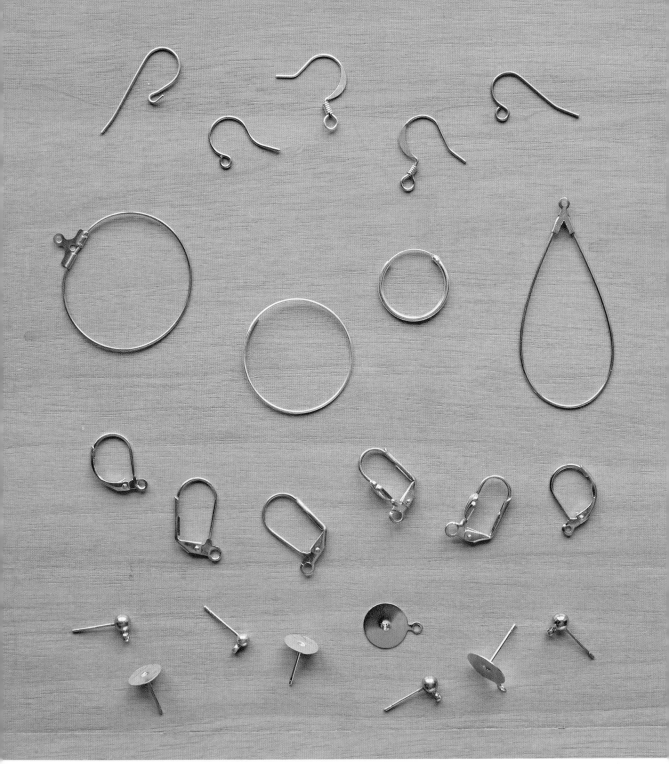

Earring findings, from top: earring wires, hoops, leverback earring components, post findings.

Bracelet Findings

Don't feel limited to making chain or beaded bracelets. Bases for cuffs, bangles, and hinge bracelets are now available at most bead shops. Look for brass cuffs, which have enough flexibility to give you a good fit around your wrist. Cheaper metals may break when you squeeze them.

Earring Findings

The right earring findings can elevate an earring from ordinary to chic. If you have sensitivities to certain metals, invest in earring findings that won't irritate your skin, like surgical steel or gold.

EARRING WIRES, also known as French wires or fishhooks, are classic and work with most earring styles. We love ear wires with a small ball at the end to secure any dangling components. For extra security, you can add small rubber stoppers to the back of ear wires, which are invisible when worn but keep the earrings from falling off during the day.

HOOPS can be found unadorned or with small loops for attaching small hanging components. They can have post backs, leverbacks, or endless hoops in which the wire that slides through the ear slips into a hollow tube behind the ear to secure it.

LEVERBACK EARRING COMPONENTS are often used for drop earrings. A loop on the bottom of the leverback opens for attaching dangling components. With a hinged closure, they are durable and secure for day-to-day wear.

POST FINDINGS enable you to turn anything with a flat back into an earring. Most have a small pad for gluing to stones or metal components. Also known as studs, these are sold notched and the accompanying butterfly back (also referred to as a friction nut or push back) will snap into the notch, securing the post to your ear. Some post findings have a small ball or stone attached to an open loop from which you can hang chain, stones, or other components.

Ring Findings

Ring bases, or shanks, are bands with small pads used to attach an element as a focal point. While we're always partial to sized rings, the variety of adjustable ring shanks now available is impressive and worth trying. Look for a metal shank that doesn't crack or break when stretched.

Studs

Studs add a bit of toughness to statement jewelry. They are available with both screw-in and prong hardware. Use a screw-in stud for heavier materials like leather and prongs for thinner materials like fabric. We use pyramid studs in the Studded Leather Band on page 64, but studs are also available in cones, domes, and spikes.

BEADING AND STRINGING MATERIALS

Bead stringing is the act of threading beads onto a strand of wire or thread. Beaded strands can then be attached with a clasp to create a bracelet or necklace, or incorporated into a more complex design.

Beading Wire

Beading wire is a durable, flexible wire made from thin strands of stainless steel that are covered with nylon. The number of tiny wires, also known as strands, determines the flexibility of the wire. The larger the number of strands, the more flexible the wire will be. When choosing a beading wire, look at both the overall diameter as well as number of strands per wire. It's often referred to by its many brand names, such as Soft Flex, Beadalon, or Tigertail. Look for a beading wire that fits the hole in the beads you're using and is strong enough to hold their weight. Use crimp beads to attach the beaded strand to a jump ring or clasp.

Clear Nylon Cord

Clear nylon cord is less likely to fray or stretch than silk beading thread and can be secured with knots, unlike beading wire. It's well suited for stringing transparent beads and styles where you'd like to hide knotted connections, like in the Loop de Loop Necklace on page 115. When shopping, you'll find clear nylon cord is also referred to as Illusion cord or monofilament. Avoid using fishing line as it will become brittle with wear.

Elastic

Elastic is great for easy bracelet styles that can stretch, and can therefore slip on and off without a clasp. Layer strands up for a statement look. Tie your elastic up with a double knot and a dab of glue.

Silk Beading Cord

Silk beading cord is traditionally used with pearls. It's ideal for small, delicate beads and stones. It comes in a large assortment of colors and is often packaged with a beading needle attached to one end of the cord.

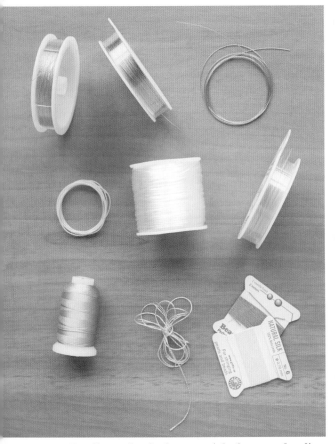

Beading and stringing materials, from top: beading wire, elastic, silk beading cord.

SEWING MATERIALS

We love incorporating nontraditional materials and techniques into our jewelry. Often we turn to sewing and embroidery materials when we design. These materials can add an unexpected element of texture or color to a piece.

Embroidery Floss

Embroidery floss is a widely used craft material because it comes in hundreds of colors to coordinate with whatever you're making. Embroidery floss is sold in skeins of about 9 yd/8 m at most craft or sewing stores. The floss can be separated into six distinct strands, so you can adjust the thickness of your thread depending on the project. Use it to attach beads to fabric or stitch layers and elements together, or on its own in a braid or tassel.

Fabric

Whether you use it as a base to stitch elements together, such as in a bib necklace, or cut it into strips for a tie-back necklace, fabric adds a soft sculptural element to your jewelry. When you're looking for fabric, pay attention to the thickness, how it moves, and if it will fray when cut. We particularly love using thin, diaphanous fabrics like chiffon and silk in jewelry.

Ribbon

Ribbon adds color, texture, and softness to jewelry that we love. It can be found at fabric and trim stores as well as many jewelry stores. Silk, cotton, velvet, linen, or any other natural fiber will be the most comfortable materials against your skin. If you're using ribbon as a tieback or to support the weight of a style, choose a thicker, heavier ribbon. If you'd like to experiment with other trims, seam binding, leather, soutache (a flat decorative braid), and braids are also available.

Sewing materials, from top: embroidery floss, fabric, ribbon.

TOOLS

The right tools for the job will
make a world of difference
when crafting statement
jewelry. Luckily, there are just
a few essential tools and they
are inexpensive and easy to
find. Some you might even
have already. While you're
shopping, try out a few sets
of pliers to find ones that feel
comfortable in your hands.

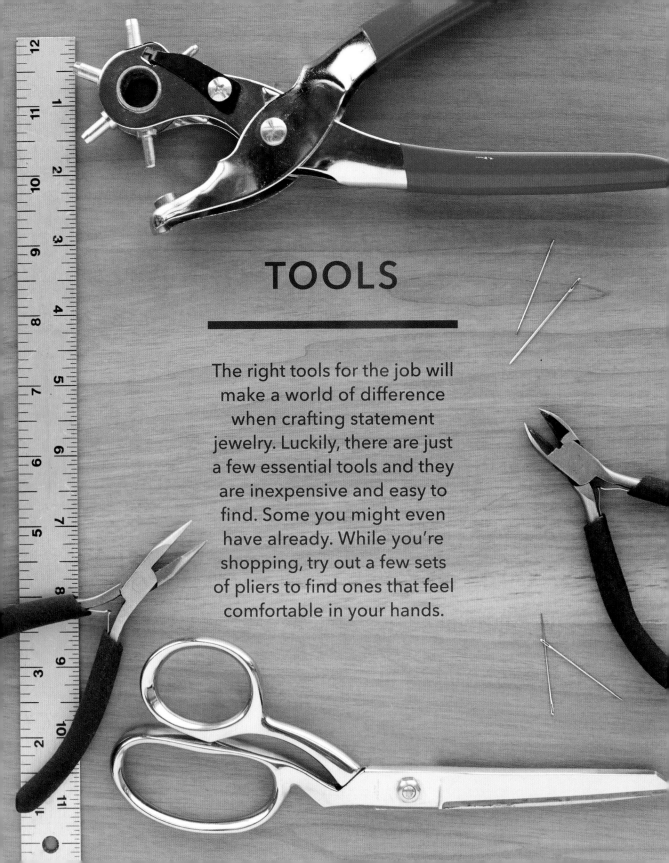

Clippers

Clippers are essential for cutting a variety of materials, and we recommend you invest in a sturdy pair. If you're doing a lot of delicate work, try a pair of **NIPPERS** to make precise, flush cuts in small places. For cutting larger chain, pick up a pair of **HEAVY-DUTY CHAIN CUTTERS**. You won't need them very often, but when you do, you'll be really glad you have them.

Pliers

There are more pliers available than you'll ever use. While some are handy to have once in a while, these are the pliers we use day in and day out:

ROUND-NOSE PLIERS are long and tapered cylinders used to create loops and curves in wire. Adjust the placement of the wire on the pliers to adjust the size of the loop. Use these for wire-wrapping and looping.

FLAT-NOSE or **CHAIN-NOSE PLIERS** are the workhorses of a jeweler. Flat-nose pliers have two flat interior surfaces and flat exterior surfaces. Chain-nose pliers have two flat interior surfaces and round exterior surfaces. Both are built for gripping components and opening jump rings. The edges are used to create angles and precise bends in wire. Avoid pliers with serrated or textured surfaces, as these tend to mar the metal. You may want to invest in two of each of these pliers, one for each hand, for opening and closing jump rings. We also use flat-nose pliers or chain-nose pliers in place of crimping pliers, since we find they work just as well.

Tools, from top: clippers, round-nose pliers, flat-nose pliers, chain-nose pliers.

Needles, from top left: beading needles, English beading needles, hand-sewing needles, wire needles.

Needles

Several types of needles are used in statement jewelry. Thin beading needles are used with thin silk or cotton thread, while hand-sewing needles are used with thicker embroidery thread. The needle you choose for a project should both fit through the hole in the bead and accommodate the thread you're using.

BEADING NEEDLES are long, thin needles used with delicate stringing materials and small beads.

ENGLISH BEADING NEEDLES look similar to a sewing needle, except for their smaller eye and thinner body.

HAND-SEWING NEEDLES are used to embroider or embellish details and can sometimes be used as an easier alternative to beading needles. We also often use these needles when using embroidery thread to connect strands of chain or beads.

WIRE NEEDLES have a larger, flexible eye that flattens when threaded through a thin bead. These tend to be easier to use than the other needles mentioned above and will work for most of the projects included in this book.

Glues and Adhesives

We use glue all the time to secure components in our pieces. There is an assortment of highly specific glues available for gluing almost any two surfaces to each other. Always read the directions carefully. Many glues require ventilation.

E-6000 glue is a thick, permanent, rubber-based bonding adhesive that's tough and flexible. Use it to attach rhinestones to metal, glass stones to metal, or beads to fabric.

SUPER GLUE is best for using as an added security measure on end caps and rhinestone ends. Flat or heavy components tend to shear off when affixed with Super Glue, so use it only with lighter materials.

TACKY GLUE is used to stop ribbon, cord, or fabric from fraying.

CLEAR NAIL POLISH stops fraying of thin beading materials and thread knots. The clear nail polish you probably have around the house works well.

TECHNIQUES

With these basic techniques, you'll not only be on your way to making each of the projects in this book, but you'll also gain the knowledge needed to design and create your own projects to suit your personal style. As with any craft, beading may take a bit of practice, but that moment when everything clicks is always the best part of learning a new skill. You may want to try out new techniques on scrap materials before diving into a project.

OPENING AND CLOSING A JUMP RING

1 Grasp the jump ring with two pairs of flat-nose pliers at each end of the opening. If you don't have two sets of pliers, grasp the jump ring with your pliers on one end of the opening and use your index finger and thumb on your other hand to grasp the other end of the opening. Pull one side of the jump ring toward you, while pushing the other away from you, in a north-to-south direction. Do not open a jump ring by pulling side to side, or east to west, because this will weaken the wire and make it difficult to bend it back into shape.

WIRE-WRAPPING

A wire-wrapped loop is one of the most secure ways to connect beads and findings. You'll need a bead with a vertical hole, a headpin, chain-nose pliers, round-nose pliers, and clippers. Choose a headpin that is at least 1 in/2.5 cm longer than the bead.

Ⓐ

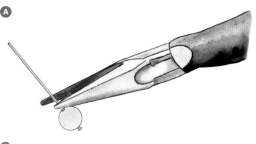

1 Thread the headpin into the bead, and with the tip of the chain-nose pliers, hold the wire directly above the bead. Ⓐ

2 Bend the wire at a 90-degree angle with your fingers. Ⓑ

continued

Ⓑ

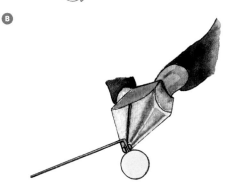

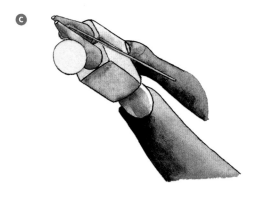

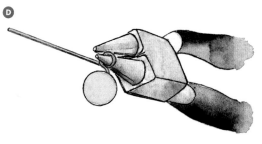

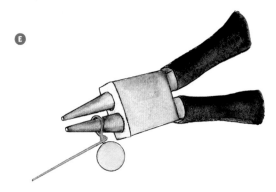

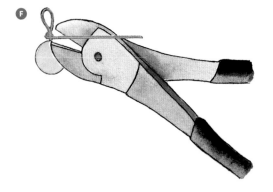

3 Grasp the space inside the bend with round-nose pliers. With your fingers, pull the wire around the round-nose pliers so that the wire is pointing down. **C**

4 Pivot the round-nose pliers in your hand, so that the bottom tip is now on the top of the loop. Continue pulling the end of the wire to complete the loop. **D**

5 Holding the loop with chain-nose pliers, tightly wrap the loop around the wire in between the loop and the bead. Wrap until you've reached the bead, usually two or three times. **E**

6 Snip the excess wire with clippers, and tuck the end into the wrapped wire with your chain-nose pliers so it doesn't catch on anything. **F**

LOOPING

Looping is the best way to connect elements to both ends of a bead, rather than just one end, like with a headpin. You'll need a bead with a vertical hole, an eye pin (or a headpin), chain-nose pliers, round-nose pliers, and clippers. Choose an eye pin that is at least 1 in/2.5 cm longer than the bead. If you don't have an eye pin on hand, you can create one by making a loop on one end of a piece of wire.

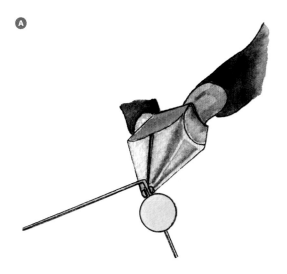

A

1 Slip the eye pin (or a headpin) through the hole in the bead. Cut the wire, leaving a tail poking out of the bead. With chain-nose pliers, fold the wire at a right angle above the bead. **A**

2 With the round-nose pliers, hold the end of the tail and bend the wire around toward the bead, creating a loop. The size of the loop will depend on which part of the nose of the round-nose pliers you use, as well as how long your wire tail is, so adjust the size according to the component you are attaching the loop to. Snip off any excess wire using clippers. **B**

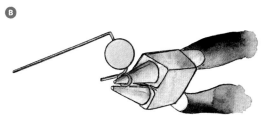

B

SECURING A CRIMP BEAD

Bead stringing is used to create long strands of beads with bead wire or thread. You'll need beading wire, beads of your choice, a clasp, and two crimp beads. Special crimping pliers are available but you can also use chain-nose pliers. Here's what to do when you are ready to attach a clasp or component.

1 Thread a crimp bead onto the end of your beading wire. Loop the wire through the small loop in the clasp and back through the crimp bead, leaving several inches/centimeters of tail at the end. **A**

2 Adjust the crimp bead so that it's close to the clasp but the clasp has enough room to move freely. Squeeze the crimp bead with chain-nose pliers to flatten the bead around the two strands of wire. **B**

3 Add beads to the beading wire, covering both the long piece of wire and the tail for the first few beads. When you're ready to end the string of beads on the opposite end of the wire, repeat this process. This step will determine the length of the bead strand, and how tight it is, so take a moment to adjust the tension when you're adding the final crimp bead. Hold the clasp with one hand and pull the tail end of the wire with the chain-nose pliers to tighten. **C**

MAKING BEADS WITH POLYMER CLAY

Polymer clay beads give you the look of ceramic beads and allow you to customize the shape, size, and texture of the beads. You'll need a cookie sheet, a glass with a flat bottom, an oven, a plastic drinking straw, and wax paper or parchment paper. Once you've baked the polymer clay, it's easy to add color to the exterior of the beads with paint, nail polish, or gold leaf.

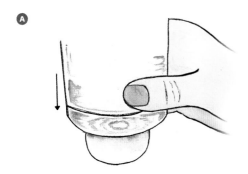

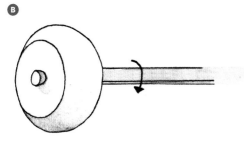

1 Break off a piece of polymer clay that is approximately the size of the bead you want to make. Roll the clay in your palms until it warms up and becomes malleable. To make a donut bead like the one shown here, roll the clay into a sphere and then flatten the sphere on two sides with a drinking glass or other flat, even surface. **A**

2 Push a plastic straw through the center of the clay to create a hole. To remove the straw cleanly, twist it as you pull it out. **B** Place the bead on a cookie sheet lined with wax paper or parchment paper.

3 Bake the bead in a preheated oven according to the package directions, usually 30 minutes at 275°F/130°C for every ¼ in/6 mm thickness.

FINISHING A RHINESTONE CHAIN

Rhinestone chain is a sparkly addition to any piece of statement jewelry, but it requires a bit of extra hardware to connect it to other elements. A crimp end makes this easy work. You'll need two crimp ends and chain-nose pliers.

1 Place the last crystal of the rhinestone chain in the open side of a crimp end. **A**

2 Press each prong over the crystal with chain-nose pliers, or press the prongs against a hard surface. The prongs will hold the crystal stone in place. **B**

3 Repeat steps 1–2 with the second end of the chain.

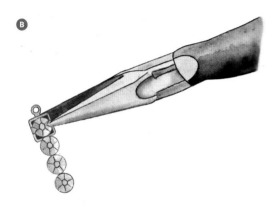

TURNING (ALMOST) ANYTHING INTO A CHARM

You may have a stash of ready-to-use charms on hand, or there might be a particularly pretty object you'd like to incorporate into your jewelry but aren't sure how. Luckily, most objects can be turned into charms and then added to your accessories.

An object needs one of two things to become a charm: a loop or a hole. Add a jump ring to anything with a loop and it's ready to attach to your piece of choice. Add a headpin and a jump ring to anything with a hole. Thread the headpin through the hole in the object and attach it to the jump ring. The jump ring attaches to a link in your piece and provides

movement so the charm has room to hang freely from your charm necklace or bracelet. By drilling a small hole and adding a headpin and a jump ring, you can turn almost anything into a charm. For brooches, hatpins, and post earrings, simply trim the pin back or post and use the shortened wire to create a loop. Then add a jump ring, and attach.

DETERMINING LENGTH

The fit of a necklace or bracelet largely depends on how long you make your piece. Since you're making the pieces yourself, you can ensure that they hit exactly where you'd like them to with a little advance preparation.

To determine **BRACELET LENGTH**, measure the diameter of your wrist with a tape measure or a piece of chain at the spot where you'd like to wear the bracelet. With chain styles, you can usually add or subtract links to adjust the bracelet fit. Most women's bracelets you'll find in stores have a wrist measurement that ranges from 6.5 to 7 in/16.5 to 17 cm long.

For each of the necklace styles in this book, we provide guidelines on the **NECKLACE LENGTH**, but when making your own jewelry, you can simply adjust the length to fit your body. You may want to hold the chain up to yourself to see where and how it falls, before cutting to the length specified in the project.

PROJECTS

EARRINGS

The first earrings were probably simply what the name implies: rings that passed through the earlobes. Earring options have evolved over time from simple studs to classic geometric hoops and stunning over-the-top drop earrings. Fortunately, earrings are often the easiest type of jewelry to make. Sometimes one or two elements are all you need to make a pair of stylish statement earrings. Once you try a few of the techniques in this section, you'll likely design your own earrings to complement your mood and your outfit. If you have sensitive skin, you may want to stick with gold, silver, or surgical stainless-steel components, since brass, copper, and nickel can cause inflammation.

Chained Posts

WE THINK EVERYDAY CLASSIC STYLES deserve the statement treatment, too. These long, graceful earrings are lovely in a pair and slightly seductive on their own or in a higher earring hole. The trick to the sleek look of these earrings is using a bead or finding that has a top-drilled hole like these triangles. This allows you to slide a jump ring through the hole to attach it directly to the chain. A variation on this is to pick up a pair of studs that have a jump ring already attached to the setting. These are available preset with a variety of stones or metal balls.

MATERIALS

5 in/12 cm flat silver cable chain, 2 mm

4 small silver jump rings

2 silver top-drilled triangle beads, 6 mm wide × 6 mm long

2 butterfly earring backs

2 silver post findings with 3-mm-dia. pad

TOOLS

Ruler

Clippers

Chain-nose pliers

E-6000 glue

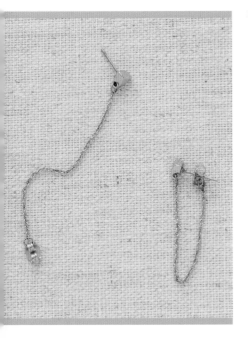

1 Cut the cable chain in half.

2 Using the chain-nose pliers and a small jump ring, attach one end of the chain to the triangle bead.

3 Attach the other end of the chain to one of the loops in the butterfly back component.

4 Flip the triangle over so it's wrong-side up on the work surface. Add a dab of E-6000 glue to the back of the triangle and place the pad of the earring post on it. Press firmly and hold in place until tacky.

5 Repeat steps 2–4 for the second earring.

6 Let the earrings dry overnight before wearing.

Stone Trellis Spikes

THESE EARRINGS ARE OUR GO-TO STYLE for when you want to make a statement at work but still keep it professional. They add character without feeling too young and they look amazing with a blazer. They use chip beads, which are an inexpensive way to incorporate semiprecious stones into your work. Chip beads are small, non-uniform slices of stone and are available in a variety of colors and materials. We love the way chalky jade looks with the shine of the brass in this style. Make these earrings your own by using tear-drop, rectangular, or even round beads.

MATERIALS

10 chip beads with top-drilled holes

6 in/15 cm gold wire, 22 gauge

4 gold square bars with loops on each end, 2 mm wide × 27 mm long

2 medium gold jump rings

2 gold leverback earring components

TOOLS

Ruler

Clippers

Round-nose pliers

Chain-nose pliers

INSTRUCTIONS

Arrange the chips

1 Arrange the chip beads into 2 sets of 5 on the work surface. If there are larger chips, place them in the center so that the beads form a V-shape.

Connect the bars

2 Cut a 3-in/7.5-cm piece of gold wire, and wire-wrap it to the bottom loop on the first bar (see wire-wrapping, page 33).

3 Thread the chips onto the wire, and wire-wrap the other end of the wire to the bottom loop on the second bar.

4 Repeat steps 2–3 for the second set of chips, for the second earring.

Attach to the top

5 Open a jump ring and slip the tops of the two connected bars onto it, then add the leverback component to the jump ring. Close the jump ring to secure.

6 Repeat step 5 for the second earring.

If you can't find bars, or want to make them a specific length, make your own bars with gold wire. Thick square wire will give these earrings the same architectural feel. Just cut them to size and use round-nose pliers to create a loop on each end to connect them.

TIP

Long Tassel Posts

LONG AND LINEAR BUT LIGHT AS A FEATHER, these earrings show movement in a slinky date-night kind of way. With just the right amount of flounce, they look especially elegant against swept-up hair. In such a long tassel, embroidery thread and cord tend to kink, so make your tassels using premade fringe found at most sewing stores. If shoulder dusters are too dramatic for your taste, trim the tassels to a more demure length. When choosing a filigree component, look for one that is slightly smaller than the carnelian teardrop component, with a hole in the filigree that is large enough to attach a jump ring.

MATERIALS

2 gold headpins

2 gold end caps, 5 mm dia. × 11 mm long

12 in/30.5 cm of 6-in/15-cm chainette fringe

2 imitation carnelian teardrops, 13 mm wide × 13 mm long

2 small gold filigree components, roughly the same size and shape as the imitation carnelian teardrops

2 gold posts with butterfly backs

2 small gold jump rings

TOOLS

E-6000 glue

Ruler

Scissors

Clippers

Round-nose pliers

Chain-nose pliers

Make the tassels

1 Slide a headpin into an end cap, and add a small dot of glue to the interior of the end cap.

2 Cut 1 in/2.5 cm of chainette fringe and tightly roll it up. Twist the roll into the end cap until it's snugly secure in the cap.

3 Use the headpin to create a wire-wrapped loop on top of the end cap.

4 Repeat with the second tassel.

Make the top

5 Place a teardrop face-down on the work surface and add an even layer of glue to the back. Add a filigree component so that one hole in the filigree is exposed at the wide end of the teardrop. This will allow you to connect the teardrop to the tassel.

6 Place the pad of the post on the filigree compo-nent, toward the top of the teardrop, making sure it's touching some of the glue that leaked through the filigree component.

7 Repeat steps 5–6 for the second teardrop. Let the posts dry overnight.

Connect the parts

8 Open a small jump ring and connect the filigree peeking out below the teardrop post to the wire-wrapped loop at the top of the end cap above the fringe. Close the jump ring to secure it.

9 Repeat step 8 for the second earring.

Geometric Hoops

HOOPS DON'T HAVE TO BE CIRCLES. These geometric hoops are a great update to the classic round look. Using square wire will make your earrings look architectural and modern while round hammered wire will look delicate and organic. A gold-filled or sterling wire will give your hoops a luster that you won't find with plated or imitation metals and will keep your earlobes from having any sensitive reaction. Just practice with a bit of inexpensive brass wire before you use your fancy gold.

MATERIALS

12 in/30.5 cm gold half-hard square wire, 20 gauge

TOOLS

Ruler

Clippers

Round-nose pliers

Chain-nose pliers

Fingernail file or sandpaper

INSTRUCTIONS

Shape the wire

1 With the clippers, cut two 6-in-/15-cm-long pieces of the square wire.

2 With the round-nose pliers, grip one end of one wire piece $\frac{1}{16}$ in/4 mm from the end and fold the wire back onto itself, creating a U-shape. This will become the catch—it will hold the part of wire that goes through your ear piercing in place.

3 With the chain-nose pliers, grip the wire about 2 in/5 cm down from the U-shape you just made, and bend the wire to the right at a 45-degree angle.

4 Now create the point at the bottom center of the earring. With the chain-nose pliers, grip the wire ½ in/1 cm away from the previous bend, and bend the wire up and to the right to make a 90-degree angle.

5 With the chain-nose pliers, make a 45-degree angle in the wire ½ in/1 cm up from the point you just made. This bend will be symmetrical to the first bend.

Make the post

6 Now make the post of the earring, which will pierce the ear, by bending the wire to fit under the U-shaped catch. With the chain-nose pliers, grip the wire 2 in/5 cm up from the previous bend, bend the wire toward the U at a 90-degree angle, and tuck it under the U-shaped catch.

7 Adjust the angles of the earring with your fingers as needed. If there are any kinks or uneven sections of wire, straighten them out by gently clamping down on the wire with chain-nose pliers. This will also work-harden the metal, making the piece stronger.

8 Trim the post end of the wire so that there is at least a ⅛-in/3-mm section of wire beyond the U-shaped catch.

9 Use a fingernail file or sandpaper to taper and smooth this end of the wire so that the earring is comfortable in your earlobe.

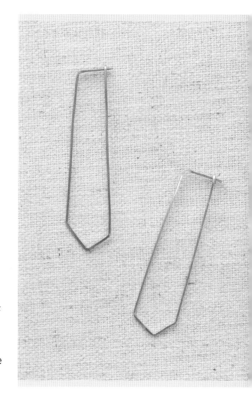

TIP

For geometric hoops, make both simultaneously to ensure that they're symmetrical. Draw out the shape you'd like to make and use it as a template. With chain-nose pliers, make each bend or curve in both earrings before moving on to the next bend. You can also gently grip both wires with the pliers to match up the angles as you work.

Mix-and-Match Drops

GRANDMA UNDERSTOOD THE BEAUTY in all those crazy clip-on earrings. Even if you have pierced ears, using clip-on components on large or heavy earrings will help you avoid discomfort and the possibility of stretching out or even tearing your earlobes. The contrast of oversize translucent crystal stones, opaque drops, and metal flowers makes for an eclectic mix in these stunning earrings. Their effortless fanciness makes them ideal for brunch with the girls. When shopping for filigree components, look for ones that are slightly smaller than the rectangular stone and have a hole large enough to fit a jump ring through.

MATERIALS ▬▬▬▬▬▬▬▬▬▬

2 rectangular blue crystals,
18 mm wide × 13 mm long

2 small gold filigree pieces

1 pair of gold clip-on
earring backs

2 medium gold filigree pieces

2 gold flower components

2 small gold jump rings

2 green teardrop beads,
14 mm wide × 28 mm long

6 in/15 cm gold wire,
28 gauge

TOOLS ▬▬▬▬▬▬▬▬▬▬

Small piece of plastic

Beacon's Glass, Metal & More
Glue

Clippers

Chain-nose pliers

Round-nose pliers

TIP Bead shops and jewelry supply stores often sell metal petal and flower stampings. You may need to layer a few petals together to make a pretty, lush flower. Alternately, look for floral components online by searching for vintage floral earrings or vintage floral clip-ons. There are thousands available from the 1950s and 1960s for just a few dollars in metal, crystal, or enamel.

INSTRUCTIONS

Make the clip-on top

1 Cover the work surface with a piece of plastic (a bead store baggie works well). Place one of the rectangular blue crystals facedown on the work surface and glue one small filigree piece to the back, making sure a small hole in the filigree is exposed on the bottom end. You'll use the hole in the filigree to attach a jump ring that will connect the top of the earring to the flower, so ensure that the filigree piece is centered on the bottom of the stone.

2 Add a thin layer of glue to the clip-on earring back and press it onto the filigree piece, clip side up.

3 Repeat steps 1–2 for the other earring. Let dry overnight.

Make the flower center

4 Holding the petals in one hand, add Beacon's glue to the back. Place the filigree component onto the petals and press into the glue. Make sure there is a place exposed and free of glue at the top center and bottom center of the filigree piece to add a jump ring, because you'll want to connect the three pieces of the earring directly above each other vertically.

5 Repeat step 4 for the other earring. Let dry overnight.

Connect the pieces

6 With the chain-nose pliers, use a small jump ring to connect the filigree piece attached to the flower component to the filigree piece attached to the clip-on earring back.

7 Using the round-nose pliers, with the gold wire, wire-wrap the green teardrop bead to the filigree piece at the bottom of the flower.

8 Repeat step 7 for the second earring.

Filigree Chandeliers

THE PALETTE OF IRIDESCENT AND PALE BLUE STONES creates an icy glow in these chandelier earrings. A quirky mix of shiny gems and opaque stones, these earrings are as easy to make as gluing stones to a base. The filigree piece can be a canvas for your wildest color combinations. Use a glue like Beacon's Glass, Metal & More Glue that doesn't harden immediately, giving you time to adjust the layout of each crystal as you go.

MATERIALS

- 2 gold oval filigree components, 1 in/30 mm wide × 1³⁄₄ in/4.5 mm long
- 2 crystal pear-shaped beads, 8 mm wide × 13 mm long
- 2 square light blue faceted stones, 10 mm
- 8 black diamond marquise stones, 4 mm wide × 15 mm long
- 4 crystal marquise stones, 4 mm wide × 15 mm long

- 2 round milky iridescent stones, 6 mm dia.
- 2 opaque blue rectangular beads, 5 mm × 8 mm
- 2 round milky light blue stones, 4 mm dia.
- 1 pair of gold earring French wires

TOOLS

- Small piece of plastic
- Beacon's Glass, Metal & More Glue
- Chain-nose pliers

INSTRUCTIONS

Arrange the crystals

1 On the work surface, lay an oval filigree component on a piece of plastic (a small bead bag works great). Add a thin layer of glue to one of the pear-shaped stones and place it at the center of the filigree. The glue will seep through the holes in the filigree and the plastic will allow you to peel the filigree piece from the work surface while the glue is tacky. Repeat for the second earring.

2 Add glue to a square stone and place it above the pear-shaped stone. Repeat for the second earring.

3 Add glue to 4 of the black diamond and 2 of the crystal marquise stones and place them, alternating dark, light, dark, in a chevron pattern, on either side of the pear-shaped stone. Repeat for the second earring.

4 Add Beacon's glue to one of the round milky iridescent stones and place it on the bottom edge of the filigree piece. Repeat for the second earring.

5 Add glue to the underside of one of the opaque blue rectangular beads and place it above the blue square stone.

6 Add the round milky light blue stone directly above the rectangular bead. Repeat for the second earring.

7 Let dry overnight.

Add French wires

8 Using the chain-nose pliers, open the loop in one of the French wires and attach it to the top of the oval filigree piece. Close the loop. Repeat for the second earring.

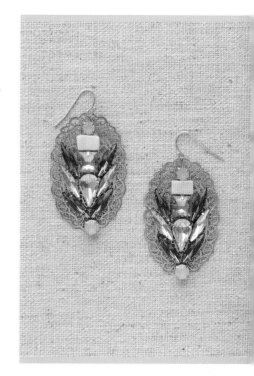

Use a toothpick or paper clip to easily add small amounts of glue to small surfaces.

BRACELETS

Bracelets can be the most expressive pieces of jewelry you wear. They reflect light as you gesture with your hands over dinner. The clink of a stack of bracelets means you're seen *and* heard. Included in this section are casual styles that make a statement, such as a leather band studded with pyramids and a braided cuff, as well as styles suited for a black tie affair, like an embellished stone cuff. Wear a few different styles together for a serious statement.

Studded Leather Band

WITH GEOMETRIC GOLD STUDS AND A BLUSH LEATHER BAND, this studded leather bracelet manages to feel feminine. In place of a snap, the closure is a dainty buckle, making this a rocker-chic staple with some delicacy. Try layering several different bracelets that have different studs or leathers.

MATERIALS

1 leather strip, ¼ in/6 mm wide × 10 in/25 cm long

Gold buckle, 10 mm wide × 15 mm long

2 ft/61 cm white thread

4 square gold screw-in pyramid studs, 8 mm

TOOLS

Ruler

Scissors

Leather punch

Sewing needle

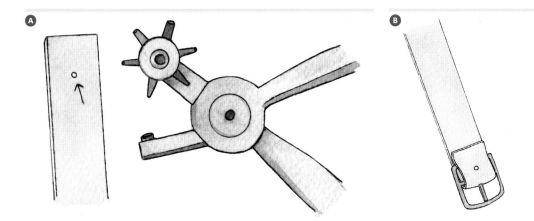

INSTRUCTIONS

Attach the buckle

1 Cut the leather about 2½ in/6 cm longer than the length of the bracelet you'd like.

2 Using a leather punch, punch a centered 2 mm hole in the leather strap 6 mm from one end. With the right side of the leather strap facing up, thread the prong of the buckle through the hole and fold the leather over the center bar of the buckle.

3 Holding the folded leather strap in one hand, use the leather punch to punch through both layers of leather in order to make two additional holes in the leather strap at once. These holes should be 5 mm from the first one. **B**

4 Thread the needle with the white thread and pull it up through the hole in both layers of leather. Tie a double knot around both layers of leather to secure the thread to the leather strips.

5 Pull the thread up through the hole and around both layers to the right, and then up through the hole and around both layers to the left. Repeat about 10 times to securely sew the buckle to the end of the leather band. Knot the thread, and trim any excess thread. **C**

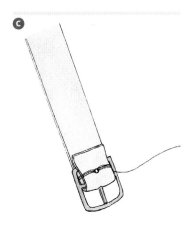

Create adjustment holes

6 Make three holes at the opposite end of the leather band. Punch the first hole 6 in/15 cm away from the buckle, then punch a second hole ¼ in/6 mm from the first hole, toward the end of the band, and punch a third hole ½ in/1 cm from the first hole. If needed, add additional holes, based on your wrist size.

7 For a finished look, with scissors, trim the end of the leather band into a smooth curve.

Attach the studs

8 By folding the leather band, find the center point between the buckle and the adjustment holes. Punch a centered hole ⅛ in/4 mm from the folded center, on the right side. Measure ⅓ in/8 mm to the right of the hole you just punched and punch another centered hole through the leather band. Repeat on the left side of the folded center point. You will have 4 holes total.

9 To attach a stud, push the back of the screw up through the suede side of the leather band, then screw on the pyramid stud.

10 Tighten and repeat with the remaining 3 studs.

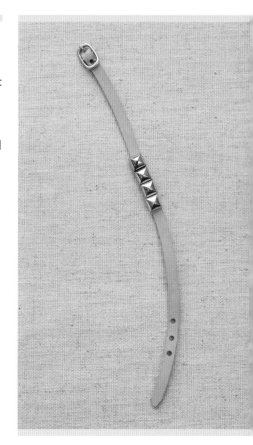

Braided Cuff

THE BRIGHT PINK, PEACH, AND MINT colors in this bracelet pack a tropical punch. The lush braid and slick brass cuff create an organic, surf vibe. Changing up the colors and width of the cuff will give this piece a whole different look. For a chic, everyday piece, use a mix of soft, tonal colors and a skinnier cuff, or try a solid primary color and an even wider cuff for a nautical look.

MATERIALS

2 skeins of magenta embroidery floss

1 skein of peach embroidery floss

1 skein of orange embroidery floss

1 skein of mint embroidery floss

1 brass wrist cuff base, 15 mm wide

TOOLS

Ruler

Scissors

Super Glue

Make the braid

1 Reserve a 1-yd/1-m length of mint embroidery floss. Unwind all the other skeins of embroidery floss and fold each one in half, doubling the thickness. Add together, creating a bundle of thread skeins.

2 With the reserved mint floss, about 1 in/2.5 cm from the folded end, wrap the bundle of skeins several times. Tie a knot in the wrapped floss and trim the excess.

3 Separate the strands of embroidery floss into three sections, each with a mix of colors. Braid the sections together until you have a braid long enough to cover the brass cuff.

4 Wrap the other end of the braid with more of the reserved mint floss, tie a knot, and trim the ends of the braid, leaving a 1-in/2.5-cm tail.

Attach the braid

5 Center the braid on the cuff and add a small dab of Super Glue in several places along the top side of the cuff to attach the braid.

6 With the remaining reserved mint floss, wrap the braid to the cuff at the ends, covering the two spots where you've already wrapped it. Triple-knot the wrapped floss on the underside of the cuff and trim the excess. Dot the knot with a dab of Super Glue for extra security. Let the braid end flow for a beach-ready look.

Gemstone Cobra Knot

WHILE WORKING ON PIECES FOR THIS BOOK, we were excited about incorporating some of our treasured finds into projects that look and feel like fine jewelry. These delicate emerald stones are luxe but, because of their size and rough facets, they are inexpensive and easy to find at your local bead shop. Other tiny gemstones like garnet, amethyst, or pearls would be lovely in this style, but we recommend sticking to a natural stone. With the simple styling and gossamer-like silk thread, the stones stand out.

MATERIALS

28 emerald rondelles,
   2 mm wide × 4 mm long

4 gold nugget beads,
   2 mm wide × 3 mm long

1 skein (2 yd/2 m) of navy
   silk beading thread with
   attached needle, size 4

TOOLS

Ruler

Scissors

Tape

Tacky Glue or other
   fabric glue

INSTRUCTIONS

Thread the beads

1 On the work surface, separate all the beads into 5 groups. Mix the gemstone rondelles with the metal nuggets for a loose, organic feel.

2 Unwind the skein of silk beading thread and use the attached needle to thread the stones onto the silk thread. Since the needle is attached to the silk thread and cannot be rethreaded, thread all of the 5 groups of beads at the same time before you cut any of them off the skein.

Cut your thread

3 Once you are happy with your bead layout, cut the first section of beads, strung onto the first 10 in/25 cm of thread, from the skein.

4 Cut each of the other 4 beaded sections off the skein, each strung onto 10 in/25 cm of thread.

Arrange strands

5 On the work surface, line up each 10-in/25-cm strand and center the beads on each one. Knot the end of each strand together so that each of the 5 strands are attached.

6 Arrange the strands into a circle, with the ends of the strands overlapping. Tape all 10 overlapping strand ends to your work surface to hold them in place.

continued

continued

TIP

A cobra knot is a great closure technique to have in your back pocket. Use it on cord or leather bracelets, or to adjust the length of long beaded necklaces. If you're using synthetic cord or thread, run a flame quickly over the ends to singe, then press the melted ends into the cobra knot to secure instead of using glue.

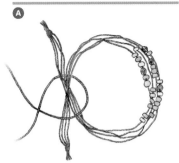

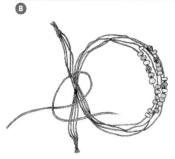

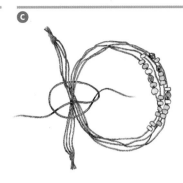

Create the closure

7 Now you will use some of the remaining silk thread to create a sliding knot or cobra knot closure for the bracelet. Place the thread under and perpendicular to the 10 taped strands.

8 Pull the right-hand side of the single working thread over the center strands and under the left side of the opposite end of the working thread. **A**

9 Pull the top thread from your left over to the right, running it under the center strands. **B**

10 Pull the thread through the loop you created and pull both sides to secure the knot. **C**

11 Repeat the knot, reversing the order. Take the thread on the left and move it over the 2 center strands of thread and under the thread on the right. Pull the thread up through the loop you just created.

12 Repeat these 2 passes 5 times.

13 Place a dab of glue onto the last pass and the thread excess. You want to glue the excess thread to the cobra knot surrounding the thread strands, but not use so much glue that the cobra knot glues to the strands of thread. Let dry for at least 1 hour.

14 Trim the excess thread once the glue has hardened. Remove the tape. Pull the ends of the closure to tighten or loosen the bracelet to fit your wrist.

Maltese Cross Cuff

COCO CHANEL WORE A PAIR OF JEWELED CUFFS day and night. She had a jeweler remove the stones from jewelry she'd been given over the years and gave them new life on a pair of Maltese cross cuffs. These coordinating cuffs became a part of her signature style and this look is still chic seventy years later. We updated this iconic style with brass and bright jewel tones. With a mix of royal blue, fuchsia, and amethyst stones it adds a classic vintage feel to any outfit. No need to layer on any other jewelry—just throw on a coat.

MATERIALS

2½-in/6-cm wrist cuff base

1 blue emerald cut stone, 18 mm wide × 25 mm long

2 black diamond baguette stones, 4 mm wide × 15 mm long

4 light amethyst octagon stones, 10 mm wide × 15 mm long

4 square crystal stones, 8 mm

4 fuchsia pear-shaped stones, 8 mm wide × 15 mm long

4 black diamond marquise stones, 15 wide mm × 8 mm long

2 crystal marquise stones, 15 mm wide × 8 mm long

2 jet pear-shaped stones, 13 mm wide × 8 mm long

TOOLS

E-6000 glue

INSTRUCTIONS

1 To set the stones in the pictured layout, start from the center and work outward. Add a thin layer of glue to the back of the blue emerald-cut stone and place it in the center of the cuff. Use a small amount of glue for each stone so that you are not dripping or smearing it. If components start moving around, hold them in place with your finger or with a toothpick for a moment until the glue gets tacky and holds the stones.

2 Glue the 2 black diamond baguettes to the top and bottom of the emerald cut stone.

3 Glue the 4 light amethyst octagons to the four longest exposed sides of the central emerald cut stone and the adjacent baguettes.

4 Maneuver the 4 square crystal stones into the spaces between the baguettes and the light amethyst octagons, and glue into place.

5 Glue down the 4 fuchsia pear-shaped stones between the crystal and the light amethyst stones on the top and bottom of the arrangement, pointed-side out.

6 Glue the 4 black diamond marquise stones in the space between the light amethyst octagons and the crystal squares on the sides of the arrangement.

7 Glue the crystal marquise stones in the space between the black diamond marquise stones.

8 Finally, glue the 2 jet pear-shaped stones facing outward on the far sides of the arrangement. These two stones may need to be held in place for a moment while the glue dries, since they are on the side of the cuff. Wait at least 24 hours for the glue to fully dry before wearing.

Use this illustration as a guide when you lay out the stone embellishments.

Classic Charm

WHEN YOU ADD CHARMS YOU LOVE—or better yet, create your own—a charm bracelet can become an instant heirloom. Choose a mix of metal and colorful charms in a variety of sizes so that the piece feels fresh and young. Collect and create charms throughout your travels or before a big event. This could be an incredibly thoughtful graduation gift or thank-you for your bridesmaids. You can never have too much luck! Charms that signify good luck include: horseshoes, four-leaf clovers, pickles, elephants, and evil eyes.

MATERIALS

Medium brass jump rings

6½-in/16.5-cm brass chain, 12 mm thick

Large brass toggle clasp

Several charms you love

TOOLS

Flat-nose pliers

Ruler

Clippers, preferably for heavy chain

Attach the clasp

1 Using flat-nose pliers, attach a medium jump ring to one end of the chain. Attach the ring end of the toggle clasp to the jump ring.

2 Measure the chain, including the toggle ring, around your wrist. Women's bracelets generally range in length from 7 in/17 cm to 8 in/20 cm. Cut to the appropriate length for your wrist with jewelry clippers.

3 Attach the bar end of the toggle clasp with another jump ring on the opposite end of the chain.

Add the charms

4 Lay out the charms next to the chain on the work surface to determine where you'd like to place each one. Space them out so there is an interesting variety of metal, color, and sizes positioned around the chain.

5 Working from one end of the chain to the other and using the flat-nose pliers, attach the charms by connecting them to medium jump rings and attaching the jump rings to the chain. Make the bracelet as dense with embellishments as you'd like by adding more charms or beads. We love a mix of color and metal, old and new.

ACCESSORIES

Sometimes all you need is a little special something to adorn your hair, shoes, fingers, or collar. Since shoe clips, hair combs, and brooches don't need as much engineering as necklaces or bracelets, they can be especially unconventional, sculptural, or even quirky. Have fun with these pieces by playing with materials, scale, and figurative elements.

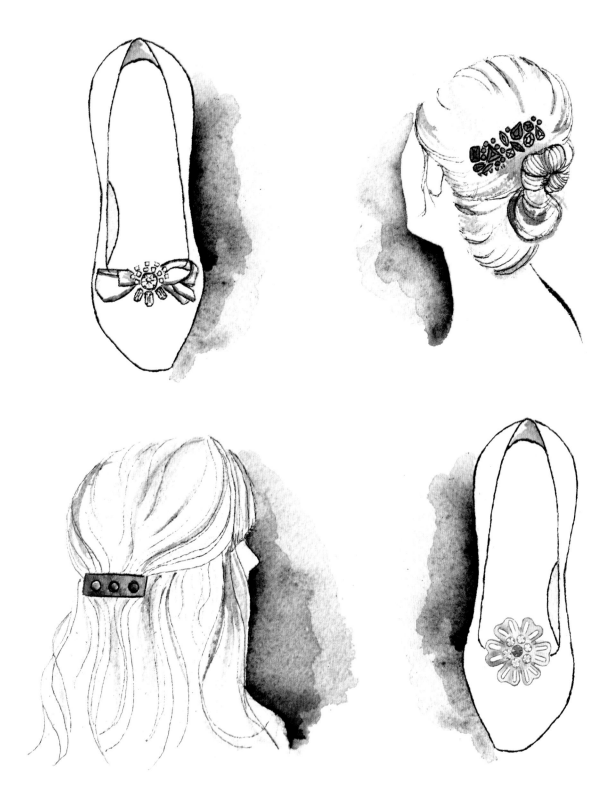

Lost and Found Vintage Ring

TURN STRAY JEWELRY PARTS, lonely earrings, or out-of-date brooches into a conversation-starting cocktail ring. Rummage through old jewelry boxes, thrift stores, or online vintage sellers for possibilities—the wackier the better. Somehow, imagery of flora and fauna or quirky stone colors look young and chic in rings, as opposed to frumpy in an outdated brooch or earring. For ensuring that the size of your object works as a ring, place it on your hand to get a sense of the scale before beginning.

MATERIALS

Vintage brooch or single
  earring

Gold ring shank with a flat pad

TOOLS

Clippers

Fingernail file or sandpaper
  (optional)

E-6000 glue

Clamp or wire (optional)

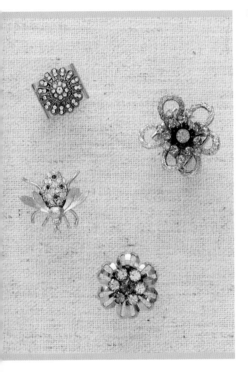

INSTRUCTIONS

Prepare your piece

1 With the clippers, remove any brooch backing, earring post, clip-on earring back, or jump rings on your vintage piece. Make sure there is a flat spot on the back of the vintage piece for gluing. If there isn't one, make one with the fingernail file or sandpaper.

Glue the components together

2 Add E-6000 glue to both the ring pad and the back of the vintage piece. Wait 10 minutes for the glue to begin curing, and then put the two pieces together. For even more security, clamp or wire them together and let the glue dry overnight.

Mod Brooch

THE SECRET TO THIS BROOCH is for you to become comfortable with a serious amount of glue. It dries clear and fills in any gaps in this mod stack of stones, so don't be shy with the glue here. Inspired by a chipped '80s shoe clip we found, this modern take on the brooch looks just right on the lapel of a camel coat or topping an extra-nubby sweater.

MATERIALS

1 oval filigree component, 20 mm wide × 25 mm long

1 jet triangle stone, 25 mm wide × 25 mm long

1 princess-cut black diamond stone, 23 mm dia.

1 square crystal stone, 10 mm wide × 10 mm long

1 long silver pin back finding, 25 mm long

TOOLS

Small piece of plastic

Beacon's Glass, Metal & More Glue

Stack the stones

1 Cover the work surface with a piece of plastic (a bead store baggie works well), and place the filigree piece on it.

2 Add a dot of glue to the underside of the jet triangular stone, and place it on the right side of the filigree piece, pointing out.

3 As you are laying out the piece, adjust the stones as needed so that they completely cover the filigree piece underneath.

4 Add a dot of glue to the underside of the princess-cut stone, and place it on the left side of the filigree piece, so the two stones are touching.

5 Add a dot of glue to the underside of the small square crystal stone, and place it so that it's resting on top of the larger stones. The pointed underside of the stone will fit between the two larger stones.

6 Wipe away any excess glue immediately. Let the glue dry overnight.

Add the pin back

7 When the glue is completely dry, peel the piece from the plastic on the work surface and flip it upside down.

8 Add a line of glue to the pin back and center it lengthwise on the oval filigree piece. Let the glue dry overnight before wearing.

Deco Hair Comb

TUCKED INTO AN UPDO AT YOUR WEDDING, this hair comb is most certainly something blue. You can use crystals you already have on hand to achieve this look. Here we used two broken clip-on earrings, several cabochons without settings, and a mix of stones in settings, some with holes for wiring and some with flat setting backs. Keep the crystals one general color and mix up the stone size, shape, and shade. Make a few of these combs to share with your bridesmaids.

MATERIALS ████████████████

Assorted crystals

Gold hair comb

1 yd/1 m gold wire, 26 gauge

TOOLS ████████████

Chain-nose pliers

Clippers

E-6000 glue

Create a layout

1 Play around with the assorted crystals to design a layout you love that fits on the hair comb. This style works best when the design looks organic like a mash-up of components in different sizes and shapes.

Attach the crystals

2 Start attaching the crystal stones that have holes or settings. To begin, with the chain-nose pliers, wrap one end of the wire around a tooth on one side of the comb several times to anchor the wire to the comb. Thread the wire through a hole or setting in one crystal and then wrap it around an adjacent tooth of the comb, securing it. Work from one side of the comb to the other. Wrap the wire around a tooth at the opposite side of the comb to anchor it again. With the clippers, snip any excess wire, and use the pliers to tuck in the sharp end.

3 Add in the other stones with dabs of glue. The glue dries slowly, so you'll have plenty of time to adjust the stones as you go.

Dance Party Shoe Clips

SHOE CLIPS AREN'T JUST FOR PROM NIGHT. Pair them with a pair of lace-up sneakers, or with a pair of pumps for a first date. The mix of deco crystal and silk ribbon adds a vintage softness and elegance we love. To make them your own, try using a bright ribbon or printed fabric instead. Don't skimp on the stitches in this project, since you'll be kicking up your heels with these.

MATERIALS

1 yd/1 m of silk ribbon, 1 in/2.5 cm wide

2 crystal components or vintage clip-on earrings

2 small silver filigree findings

Thread, in a color to match the ribbon

2 shoe clip findings

TOOLS

Ruler

Scissors

Tacky Glue

Sewing needle

E-6000 glue

INSTRUCTIONS

Make the bow

1 Cut two 15-in/38-cm lengths of silk ribbon, and tie each piece in a simple bow.

2 With one of the bows in your hand, make a sandwich, with the bow in the middle, a crystal component centered on the top, and a filigree finding centered on the bottom.

3 Tack the three layers to each other with a small dab of Tacky Glue.

4 Repeat for the second bow. Let dry overnight.

Stitch the layers together

5 Thread the sewing needle, and stitch together the three sandwiched layers of one bow—the filigree finding, ribbon, and crystal component.

6 Once the three components are secure, stitch one of the shoe clip findings to the filigree finding. These clips will get lots of wear on your shoes, so make at least 10 stitches to secure the clip to its decorative top. Shoe clips generally have two holes made just for stitching them to a surface, but if your clips don't, you can use E-6000 glue to attach them to the filigree finding.

7 Tie off the thread with a secure knot and trim any excess thread.

8 Repeat to make the second silk bow shoe clip.

NECKLACES

There is a reason humans have been making necklaces for longer than we've been writing. Sitting close to the heart, they are inherently personal. A necklace frames your face, becoming the centerpiece of an outfit. To elevate whatever we put on that morning, we keep a selection of necklaces at home and at work to throw on when heading to a meeting or out for dinner.

Necklaces are excellent vehicles for incorporating nontraditional and unexpected materials—the projects included in this section use clay, fabric, rope, stones, reworked vintage jewelry, and thread. Master a few basic necklace silhouettes and soon you'll be mixing and matching materials to design new styles.

High-Low Tie Back

WHETHER YOU WEAR IT LONG OR SHORT, with a T-shirt or a sheath, versatility is the name of the game with this necklace. A mix of industrial chain, soft ribbon, and natural stones, it fits in at the office or on the back deck. Plus, switching the ribbon on this necklace is as easy as tying and untying a knot. Try using velvet in the winter, eyelet in the spring, and silk anytime. The silk ribbon used here is hand-dyed and available in an endless variety of colors.

MATERIALS

14 in/35.5 cm of silver snake chain, 4 mm dia.

4 silver end caps with 1 loop, which fit snugly around the chain, 5 mm dia. × 8 mm long

5 stone beads with top-drilled holes, 20 mm wide × 28 mm long

1 ft/30.5 cm flexible beading wire, thin enough to thread through the bead holes

2 silver-tone crimp beads, 2 mm dia.

2 small silver jump rings

2 yd/2 m ribbon, 1 in/2.5 cm wide

TOOLS

Clippers

Ruler

E-6000 glue

Chain-nose pliers

Scissors

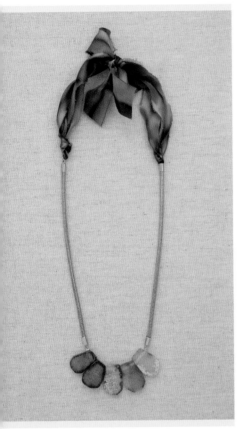

Make your own ribbon out of fabric. Use scissors or a rotary cutter to trim fabric to the desired thickness of ribbon you'd like to use for your project. This works particularly well with silk, cotton, and velvet.

INSTRUCTIONS

Connect the beads to the chain

1   With the clippers, cut the snake chain in half. Glue each of the 4 ends of the chain into an end cap. Let dry overnight.

2   Arrange the 5 stone beads in a gentle curve on your work surface.

3   Thread the 12-in/30.5-cm piece of flexible beading wire through the loop on one of the end caps, and thread both ends of the flexible beading wire through a crimp bead.

4   Thread the stones onto the flexible beading wire. Add the second crimp bead, and thread the wire through the loop on the second end cap and back through the crimp bead. With the chain-nose pliers, crimp the crimp bead, and clip any excess wire, leaving a short tail.

5   Attach a small jump ring to the loops on each of the two remaining end caps.

Add the ribbon

6   With the scissors, cut the ribbon in half. Thread one of the pieces of ribbon through a jump ring. Pull the ribbon halfway, until the jump ring is in the center of the ribbon.

7   Loosely tie a knot with the ribbon around the jump ring, covering it.

8   Repeat on the other end of the chain with the other length of ribbon. You now have 2 lengths of ribbon on each side. To wear the necklace, choose how long you want to wear it and, with the ribbon, tie a bow in the back.

Multirow Amulet

PUT THIS NECKLACE ON in the morning and you'll look effortlessly styled without having to think about layering on several necklaces. Seen together, small details like a tiny thread tassel, a vintage heart charm, a carved elephant, and a glass stone are more than the sum of their parts. This necklace is all about a variety of textures, so choose charms or stones that play off of each other. The chains we used are merely suggestions; make this necklace your own by selecting chains that work best with the charms you've chosen.

MATERIALS

1 yd/1 m embroidery floss for the tassel, color of your choice

17 small gold jump rings, plus any additional needed to create charms

4 charms, of your choice

Headpins, if any charms are missing a loop

3 stone bar connectors

17 in/43 cm gold flat cable chain, 3 mm

2 gold end bars with 2 loops on one side and 1 loop on the other

17 in/43 cm gold curb chain, 1 mm

22 in/56 cm gold tube chain, 2 mm

25 in/63.5 cm gold bar chain, 2 mm

32 in/81 cm textured gold round cable chain, 1 mm

4 medium gold jump rings

1 medium gold lobster clasp

TOOLS

1 strip of card stock, 1 in/2.5 cm wide × 2 in/5 cm long

Scissors

Chain-nose pliers

Ruler

Clippers

Round-nose pliers

INSTRUCTIONS

Make the tassel

1 Wrap the embroidery floss around the piece of card stock about 10 times, ending the last wrap on the side of the card where you started so both loose ends are on the same side; these will become part of the tassel. Cut the thread. Attach a small gold jump ring to the floss loop and close the ring with the chain-nose pliers.

2 Slide the floss bundle off the card and use a small piece of the floss about 6 in/15 cm long to tightly tie the tassel together close to the jump ring end. Secure the tie with a tight double knot. Pull the ends of the knotted tie down so they become part of the bundle.

3 With the scissors, cut through the floss loop on the opposite end from the small gold jump ring to create the tassel. Trim the tie ends even with the tassel ends.

Prepare the charms

4 If a charm is missing a jump ring, add a small gold jump ring now. If there is no loop at the top of the charm, use a headpin to create one, then add a small gold jump ring to the headpin.

5 Using chain-nose pliers, connect the 3 stone bar connectors with 2 small jump rings to create a chain segment that you'll use later.

continued

The technique for creating the tiny tassels in this necklace is surprisingly versatile. Try adding a tassel to a charm necklace, or make two and create tassel earrings. A grouping of larger tassels in slightly different shades would make an interesting soft statement necklace.

TIP

Make the chain and attach the charms

6 Attach one end of the flat cable chain to the right side of the first end bar with a small jump ring. Thread the first charm onto the chain. Connect the opposite end of the flat cable chain to the left-most end bar. Thread the first charm onto the chain. With another small gold jump ring, connect the opposite end of the flat cable chain to the leftmost loop of the end bar on the right-hand side.

7 Attach a gold small jump ring to each end of the curb chain. Attach the jump rings to the same loops on the end bars as the previous chain strand.

8 Cut the curb chain in half. Insert the chain segment you created with the three stone bar connectors in the center of this chain with 2 small jump rings.

9 Slide the second charm onto the tube chain and connect the chain to the same loops on the end bars with 2 small jump rings.

10 Slide the third charm onto the bar chain and connect the ends of the bar chain to the remaining loop on each of the end bars with 2 small gold jump rings.

11 Connect the ends of the textured round cable chain to the same loops on the end bars with 2 small gold jump rings. Add the tassel with a medium jump ring 15 in/38 cm down on one side of the chain. Attach the final charm with 2 medium gold jump rings at the center of the chain.

Add the clasp

12 Attach a medium jump ring to the end bar with a small jump ring. Attach the lobster clasp to the other end bar with a small jump ring.

Gold Bib

WITH A NECKLACE THIS SLEEK AND CHIC, there is no need for additional adornment. Inspired by chain mail and metal mesh, these metal links are substantial and no-nonsense, perfect for protecting you in a modern-day battle (think first dates and job interviews). We love it with a summery sailor shirt or peeking out from under a blazer.

MATERIALS

At least 38 large gold jump rings

At least 53 gold double-bar connectors, 13 mm long × 5 mm wide (preferably ones that have two distinct loops, one on each end)

1 gold lobster clasp

2 small gold jump rings

1 medium gold jump ring

TOOLS

2 pairs of chain-nose pliers

Ruler

Make a grid out of gold rings

1 Think of this piece as a grid of rings and connectors. To visualize the grid, on the work surface, lay out the bib section before you begin. There are 7 rings on the top 3 rows of the bib and 5 rings on the bottom row.

2 Connect the top row of rings with a bar connector between each ring. It's best to use connectors with loops on each end to ensure that the rings are held at an even distance in a grid-like formation. Slide a ring in a loop on either end of the bar connector and press the loops down with chain-nose pliers to secure.

3 Repeat step 2 until you have 3 individual rows of 7 rings and 1 row of 5 rings.

4 Lay out each row of rings so that the connectors all sit horizontally, creating a chain, and the 4 rows are atop each other in the sequence shown in the photo.

5 Connect each row vertically with additional connectors. You have completed the bib section of the necklace.

Add chain for the neck

6 Measure where you'd like the bib to fall on your neck and how long the chain to the back should be on each side. Subtract about 1 in/2.5 cm from the total length to account for added length from the clasp. For example, if you need a total of 10 in/25 cm of chain for the back of the necklace, make each chain side about 4½ in/11 cm long. Make the 2 side chains for the neck by using the same method of connecting rings with bar connectors.

7 Attach the 2 side chains to the top corner ring on each side of the bib.

8 Add the clasp to one side of the chain with a small jump ring.

9 Add the medium jump ring to the opposite side chain with a small jump ring.

Try this look in silver or hematite, or try alternating plating colors of the rings and connectors. To add a touch of softness, wrap links with thread, add stones or crystal to several connectors with glue, or use leather instead of chain in the back. **TIP**

Vintage Rhinestone Chain Mix

VINTAGE RHINESTONE NECKLACES ARE DISTINCTIVE, eye-catching, and surprisingly inexpensive. You can pick up a stash of necklaces at your local thrift store, flea market, or on eBay. On their own, these vintage wares are often too short to wear, but layer a few together, add a little length, and you have something really spectacular. For this necklace we paired the glitzy crystal chain with dark oversize curb chain to make it casual enough to wear every day. But you can use this same technique to create a sparkly style for weddings or holiday parties.

MATERIALS

- 2 rhinestone necklaces, about 15 in/38 cm long, clasps removed
- 4 hematite crimp ends that fit over the rhinestones
- 18 small silver jump rings
- 18 in/46 cm hematite curb chain, 4 mm
- 12 in/30.5 cm silver bar and link chain, 2 mm
- 24 in/61 cm antique silver curb chain, 10 mm
- 30 in/76 cm antique silver curb chain, 2 mm
- 12 in /30.5 cm silver fishbone chain, 10 mm
- 4 large silver jump rings
- 1 medium silver lobster clasp

TOOLS

- 2 pairs of chain-nose pliers
- Ruler
- Clippers

Prepare the chain

1 With the clasp removed, insert one end of a rhinestone chain into a crimp end and, using the chain-nose pliers, fold the prongs over the stone, securing the stone in the crimp end. Repeat for the opposite end of the necklace. Then repeat this step for the second rhinestone necklace.

2 With two small jump rings, one on each side, add some of the 4-mm hematite curb chain to each end of one necklace to lengthen it. How much you lengthen your necklace will depend on the length of the necklace you have on hand. You'll want one necklace to fall slightly longer than the other, creating a waterfall effect, so even if you need to add some chain to the other necklace, be sure to keep the two necklaces at different lengths.

3 Make sure each remaining chain is cut to size. The 2-mm silver bar and link chain should be cut to 12 in/30.5 cm long. Cut the 10-mm antique silver curb chain into one 12-in/30.5-cm section and two 6-in/15-cm sections. Cut the 2-mm antique silver curb chain into two 15-in/38-cm sections. If you haven't already, cut the fishbone chain so it's 12 in/30.5 cm long.

4 Set aside the two 6-in/15-cm sections of the antique silver 10-mm curb chain. Lay out the remaining chains in the order you'd like them to appear on the necklace. Vary the lengths to create a lush, layered look.

TIP *You can find inexpensive rhinestone necklaces on sites like eBay and by searching flea markets on the weekend. If you're searching online, use search terms like vintage, rhinestone, faceted, crystal, graduated, glass, necklace, emerald, sapphire, black diamond, choker, rhodium, gold tone, and plated.*

Connect the chain

5 Attach a small jump ring to each end of each chain.

6 Connect the ends of all the small jump rings onto a large jump ring. Mix up the order of the chains a bit to create a tousled look and then attach the ends of the small jump rings onto the other large jump ring.

7 Use small jump rings to attach the two pieces of reserved chain to the large jump rings. Make sure these two pieces of chain are separate from the chain jumble, because they will create the back of the necklace.

Add the clasp

8 Add the clasp to one end of the oversize chain with a jump ring and add a large jump ring to the other end of the chain.

Hanging Pendant

OUR TAKE ON A MODERN-DAY CHATELAINE, this piece can evolve and grow as you collect charms and ephemera. Worn long, it's a gathering place for new finds and gently aged heirloom jewels. Use a mix of long charms and small beads for an eclectic grouping. The bezel wire used for the bar, stretching from one end of the U-shaped wire to the other, is made from extra-soft sterling silver so it's pliable and easy to use, and the oval jump rings allow each charm or pendant to hang separately and elegantly. The wire spool of silver-toned wire should be in a circular shape when you buy it in order to reduce the amount of shaping you'll need to do to it.

MATERIALS

- 1 spool of 18-gauge silver-toned wire
- 6 in/15 cm sterling bezel wire, 5 mm
- 30 in/76 cm silver cable chain, 3 mm
- 3 medium silver jump rings
- Small silver oval jump rings (1 for each charm, plus 1 additional)
- 1 medium silver lobster clasp
- Silver headpins (one for each charm)
- Assorted charms and beads

TOOLS

- Clippers
- Round-nose pliers
- Chain-nose pliers

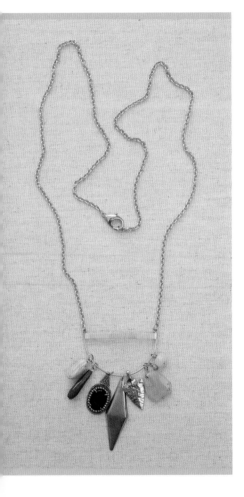

Create the wire base

1 To create the U-shape of 18-gauge silver-toned wire for this piece, cut slightly more than half of a coil from the spool. Using round-nose pliers, create a loop on either end of the wire.

2 Wrap the ends of the bezel wire around the 18-gauge wire right below each loop, creating a semicircle.

3 With chain-nose pliers, attach the loops in the bezel wire to the ends of the silver cable chain with 2 medium silver jump rings.

4 With clippers, cut the cable chain in half. Attach 1 medium jump ring to 1 end of the chain, and with a small jump ring, attach the lobster clasp to the other end of the chain.

Add the charms

5 Thread a headpin through each charm and make a loop at the top of each one. Add a small oval jump ring to each loop.

6 Connect each small oval jump ring with its charm to the 18-gauge wire U-shape.

Loop de Loop

A NECKLACE DOESN'T HAVE TO BE OVERSIZE or covered in crystals to make a statement. These beaded loops are playful and sculptural, but deceptively simple to make with just some fishing line and round beads. Make it your own by playing with the size of the beads and the loops. For a fun, casual look, pair this piece with a comfortable T-shirt and well-worn jeans.

MATERIALS

5 yd/5 m monofilament

8 light blue round beads, 14 mm dia.

1 black diamond rondelle finding, 10 mm dia. × 3 mm wide

22 aqua round beads, 12 mm dia.

4 crystal rondelle findings, 9 mm dia. × 3 mm wide

22 hunter green round beads, 12 mm dia.

49-strand bead-stringing wire

2 strands (or 100) round hunter green beads, 8 mm dia.

4 gold crimp beads, 2 mm dia.

2 medium gold jump rings

1 medium gold spring ring clasp

5 in/12 cm section of gold chain, 10 mm

TOOLS

Ruler

Scissors

Sewing needle

Chain-nose pliers

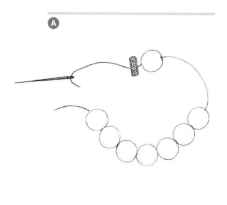

INSTRUCTIONS

Create the loop chain

1 It's easiest to work from the center loop outward. Cut a 12-in/30.5-cm length of monofilament, and thread it through the needle. Using the needle and monofilament, string the 8 light blue round beads and the 1 black diamond rondelle finding. Knot the ends of the monofilament together into a triple knot, creating a circle out of the beads. Trim any excess monofilament.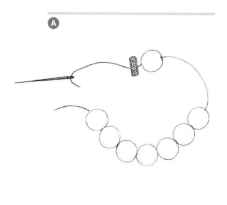

2 Cut a second 12-in/30.5-cm piece of monofilament, and thread it through the needle. Using the needle, string 11 of the aqua round beads and 1 of the crystal rondelle findings onto the monofilament, and then with these 12 strung beads, create a loop through the first (center) circle. Triple knot the monofilament and trim any excess.

3 Repeat step 2 on the other side of the light blue (center) bead circle with the remaining 11 aqua beads and with 1 of the crystal rondelle findings.

4 Cut a third 12-in/30.5-cm piece of monofilament. String 11 of the 12-mm hunter green beads, and loop the string through one of the aqua beaded circles, pulling the loop to the outside.

5 Repeat step 4: String the remaining eleven 12-mm hunter green beads through the opposite aqua bead circle, pulling the loop to the outside.

continued

Connect to the clasp

6 Cut a 12-in/30.5-cm section of bead-stringing wire. Thread one strand of the small (8-mm-dia.) hunter green beads onto the wire. Add a gold crimp bead to one end of the wire, crimp it with the chain-nose pliers, and connect it to a medium jump ring.

7 Thread the other end of the bead-stringing wire through one of the 12-mm hunter green bead loops, connect it to the same jump ring with a second crimp bead, and crimp it with the chain-nose pliers, creating a large double strand of 8-mm beads that loops through one end of the 5-circle chain.

8 Repeat steps 6–7, creating a second large loop of 8-mm hunter green beads on the opposite side of the 5-circle chain.

9 Connect the spring ring clasp to a jump ring on one side of the necklace and connect the gold chain to the other side.

Chunky Byzantine Collar

INSPIRED BY ANCIENT BYZANTINE MOSAICS, this structured collar-style necklace creates a bold line of color, which looks lovely peeking out from under a leather jacket. Using cube beads in a mix of sizes and tones shows their subtle sheen in an understated way. Selecting the appropriate end bar component is key to making this style clean and current. Choose an end bar free from ornamentation so it comfortably complements the beads you're using.

MATERIALS

1 strand of brass 4-mm cubes, at least 13 in/33 cm long

1 strand of 3-mm × 6-mm pyrite discs, at least 14 in/35.5 cm long

1 strand of 13-mm × 4-mm malachite rectangles, at least 15 in/38 cm long

1 strand of 4-mm howlite cubes, at least 16 in/40.5 cm long

1 strand of 6-mm dyed howlite cubes, at least 17 in/43 cm long

1 strand of 5-mm pyrite cubes, at least 18 in/46 cm long

6 yd/6 m of 0.024-in-/0.6-mm-thick beading wire

2 gold end bar components with 6 holes on one side and a loop on the other

12 gold crimp beads, 2 mm dia.

3 medium gold jump rings

8 in/20 cm gold link chain cut in half, 12 mm

1 medium gold spring ring clasp

TOOLS

Ruler

Clippers

Tape

Chain-nose pliers

Create the strands

1 One at a time, remove the beads from 1 of the strands and slide them onto the beading wire.

2 Measure 6 in/15 cm from the last bead and cut the wire. Tape the wire ends together to secure, and set aside.

3 Repeat steps 1–2 for the remaining 5 bead strands.

Connect bead strands to the first end bar

4 Begin connecting the wires of beads to the end bars, starting with the innermost (closest to the top) strand of beads. We used the brass beads on the inner-most strand. Remove the tape from one end of the beading wire at a time and thread it through the end bar. Attach a crimp bead to secure the wire strand, and use the chain-nose pliers to crimp the crimp bead. Repeat for the other end of the beading wire.

5 Working outward from the innermost bead strand to the outer strands, continue attaching each row to the end bar with crimp beads.

Connect bead strands to the second end bar

6 The outer strand of beads will end up about 4 in/10 cm longer than the inner row, so make sure that the inner row is the shortest before you begin connecting the strands to the second end bar.

7 Like in step 4, connect the innermost row of beads to the second end bar with a crimp bead. Lay the necklace flat on the work surface, in a curved shape, just like it would lie on your neck. Lay the next row next to the inner row, following the same curve.

8 Continue connecting the remaining bead strands to the second end bar until you have a flat, even collar shape.

continued

continued

Have a necklace that's too short? Make any necklace longer by adding several inches/centimeters of chain to the back of the clasp as a necklace extender. This adds versatility to styles by increasing the variety of necklines you can wear them with.

TIP

Attach the back chain

9 Using a medium gold jump ring, attach one 4-inch section of link chain to the ring on the top of one end bar. Repeat, attaching the other section of link chain.

10 The necklace should sit squarely on your collarbones. If the necklace is too long, cut the chain to a size that fits you.

11 Add the spring ring clasp at one end of the chain using a medium jump ring.

Soft Statement Piece

WE HAVE A NICKNAME FOR THIS STYLE AROUND THE STUDIO: ceramics teacher chic, and we can't get enough of it. The mix of prints, natural materials, and scale feels bohemian without being hippie. Making your own beads out of polymer clay is surprisingly easy and allows you to create them in any shape, size, texture, and finish. Make this style your own by playing with fabric prints, bead shapes, and colors. Pair your necklace with a long flowy dress.

MATERIALS

- 3 packages of 2 oz/55 g polymer clay to make 5 polymer clay beads (2 donut-shaped, 2 disc-shaped, and 1 barrel-shaped)
- 1 yd/1 m strip of 2-in-/5-cm-wide fabric, in a print you love
- At least 10 in/25 cm of rope, 10 mm
- 2 end caps that fit the rope end snugly

- 1 yd/1 m flexible beading wire
- 2 gold crimp beads, 2 mm dia.
- 4 hollow brass beads, 20 mm dia.
- 1 hollow brass bead, 22 mm dia.
- 1 wood bead, 20 mm wide × 30 mm long
- 2 large oval gold jump rings
- 1 large gold spring ring clasp
- 1 medium gold jump ring

TOOLS

- Flat-bottom drinking glass or another flat, even surface
- Plastic drinking straw, 5 mm dia.
- Cookie sheet
- Wax paper or parchment paper
- Ruler
- Oven
- Scissors
- E-6000 glue
- 2 pairs of chain-nose pliers
- Clippers

INSTRUCTIONS

Make the clay beads

1 To create the 2 donut-shaped beads, roll the clay into balls with your hands and flatten them slightly with a glass. The donut-shaped beads pictured are approximately 10 mm wide × 20 mm long.

2 To create the large barrel-shaped bead, roll out a log of clay and flatten it slightly with a glass. This bead measures approximately 20 mm wide × 23 mm long.

3 To create the 2 disc-shaped beads, roll the clay into balls and simultaneously pull the edges out and pinch or flatten the top and bottom inward. These beads are approximately 20 mm wide × 10 mm long.

4 Smooth out the beads with your finger and a bit of water.

5 Insert the straw into the center of each bead to create a hole. Twist the straw slightly as you remove it to make sure the bead has a smooth hole.

6 Place the beads on a cookie sheet lined with wax paper or parchment paper. Bake in the preheated oven at 275°F/135°C for about 40 minutes. If your baked bead sizes don't conform to the ones given in steps 1–3, just remember to cook 15 minutes for every ¼ in/6 mm of clay. Check on the beads about every 10 minutes. The clay should feel firm but retain its white color. Polymer clay can become brownish in color if overbaked. Remove from the oven and let cool for 1 hour.

continued

> **TIP**
>
> *For tips on making your own polymer clay beads, follow the instructions on page 37, and also see the directions on the package.*

Wrap the rope

7 Wrap the fabric strip around the rope diagonally until you've covered 8 in/20 cm of rope. Cut each end of the rope, and wrap the fabric around the rope ends so it covers all the frayed rope threads.

8 Add a dab of glue to the inside of each end cap. Twist one end of the wrapped rope into one of the end caps. If it's a tight fit, twisting the rope as you insert it will help. Repeat for the other rope end and end cap. Set the rope aside for the glue to dry, about 15 minutes.

Assemble the necklace

9 Loop the flexible beading wire through a crimp bead, through the loop on one of the end caps, and then thread the wire end back through the crimp bead. With chain-nose pliers, flatten and secure the crimp bead around both strands of the flexible wire.

10 In your desired order, string your brass, clay, and wood beads onto the flexible beading wire, covering the crimp bead.

11 Add a second crimp bead, loop the flexible beading wire through one of the large oval jump rings, and thread the wire tail back through the crimp bead. Slide the crimp bead down over both wire strands so that it's between two of the beads, and with the chain-nose pliers, crimp it around both wire strands. Clip any excess wire, leaving a small tail hidden between the beads.

12 Connect the gold jump ring clasp to the other end of the rope with the medium gold jump ring. Then clasp it to a second large oval gold jump ring attached to the end cap on the first end of the rope.

Embellished Agate

THE INTRICATE CRYSTAL EMBELLISHMENT and mix of organic and geometric natural stone of this necklace are surprisingly easy to construct. We used pyrite and agate slabs, but you can use this technique with any flat stone. Don't worry if the stones overlap when you wear it; it creates a full look around your collarbones. Be warned: once you start embellishing, you might have a hard time stopping—it's addictive!

MATERIALS

5 trapezoid agate slices, approximately 3 cm wide × 4 cm long

Mix of crystal stones in marquise, baguette, oval, round, and square shapes, ranging from 5 to 15 mm wide

22 in/53 cm gunmetal curb chain, 10 mm

30 medium gunmetal jump rings

6 in/15 cm gunmetal double curb chain, 10 mm

1 medium gunmetal spring ring clasp

1 large closed gunmetal jump ring

9 gunmetal headpins

4 slabs of pyrite, approximately 2 cm wide × 3.5 cm long

9 gunmetal beads, 2 mm dia. (used as stoppers if needed)

TOOLS

E-6000 glue

Clippers

Ruler

Chain-nose pliers

Round-nose pliers

INSTRUCTIONS

Embellish the agate slices

1 Lay out the agate slices flat on the work surface. Use the glue to embellish the agate slices with a mix of the crystal stones. Make the design on each agate slice slightly different, for a loose, organic feel. Let the glue dry overnight before continuing.

Create the chain base

2 Cut the curb chain into two lengths, one 10½ in/ 26.5 cm long and the other 11½ in/29 cm long. Place the chain lengths in a curved double row on the work surface, with the shorter piece as the inner row and the longer as the outer row. Ⓐ

3 Using chain-nose pliers, connect these two chains with medium jump rings so that they will lie flat on your neck. Start with a jump ring connecting the two centermost links and work outward, adding another jump ring every fifth link. Ⓑ

4 Using chain-nose pliers, attach a medium jump ring to the end of each row of chain for a total of 4 jump rings. Connect each jump ring to the end of the double curb chain. Ⓒ

5 Cut the double curb chain in half. Attach the spring ring clasp to one end of the double curb chain with a medium jump ring. Attach the large closed jump ring to the other end of the double curb chain with chain-nose pliers.

Attach the stone slabs and slices

6 Insert headpins into each stone (agate or pyrite) slice or slab. If the holes are larger than the head of the headpin, use a small 2-mm gunmetal bead as a stopper—just thread the small bead onto the headpin before you add the agate slice in order to keep the agate from falling off the headpin.

7 Using the round-nose pliers, create a loop at the top of each stone slab or slice and connect the headpin loops to the outer curb chain with medium jump rings. Start at the center, with an embellished agate slice. Space the stones about 1 in/2.5 cm apart, alternating between agate and pyrite.

Woven Collar

INSPIRED BY ANCIENT EGYPTIAN BROAD JEWELED COLLARS, this elegant necklace rests on your shoulders, framing your collarbone in a graceful way. In a balancing act not for the timid, the piece brings together thread, stones, chain, and crystals to make a little black dress anything but basic. When the woven collar is off duty, rest it on your dresser or on a stack of books. It deserves to be seen.

MATERIALS

- 30 in/76 cm of gold curb chain, 14 mm
- 7 skeins embroidery floss in several neutral colors
- 2 gold end caps
- 1 strand of 48 rondelle beads, at least 12 in/30.5 cm long; round beads will also work
- 10 gold headpins
- 5 crystal sew-on baguette stones in metal settings, 10 mm wide × 30 mm long
- 3 black diamond baguette stones, 20 mm wide × 7 mm long
- 1 large gold spring ring clasp
- 10 medium gold jump rings
- 1 large gold jump ring

TOOLS

- Clippers
- Ruler
- Scissors
- Sewing needle
- Super Glue
- Masking or washi tape (optional)
- Binder clip (optional)
- Chain-nose pliers
- Round-nose pliers
- E-6000 glue

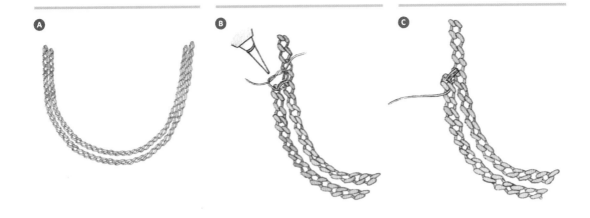

INSTRUCTIONS

Connect the chain

1 From the length of gold curb chain, cut two rows: one 17 in/43 cm long and one 12 in/30.5 cm long. Lay them out on a flat work surface in a gentle curve, as if they were resting on your shoulders. Center the shorter chain below the longer chain. **A**

2 Thread the needle with 1 full strand of embroidery floss, about 8 yd/8 m long, then fold it over itself to double it.

3 Using the very end of the thread, tie the leftmost link of the short chain to the long chain, using a triple knot. Add a dab of Super Glue to secure it. **B**

4 To use the threaded needle to lash the chains together, come from underneath the chain and through the first link. **C**

5 Wrap the thread around the first link twice. **D**

6 Move onto the next link by coming from underneath the second link and wrapping that link twice. **E**

7 Continue wrapping until you've reached the end of the shortest chain. Knot the thread, trim any excess thread, and add a dab of Super Glue to secure the knot.

Add the beads

8 To add the beads, start by knotting the thread at the same spot on the end of the short chain. Slide the end cap onto the thread, followed by the strand of rondelles. Leave this strand unknotted for now, since the length will vary. Be careful not to spill the beads at the end as you're working. You can fold a

piece of masking or washi tape over the end of the thread for extra security. **F**

9 Tie the last of the thread from that skein to the same spot and use this thread to wrap around each rondelle bead, securing them to the chain. As you go around, make sure to keep the necklace on a curve, pushing each rondelle into place. When you get to the end of the short chain, remove any excess rondelles and add the second end cap to the embroidery thread. Tie both threads to the end of the chain, cut any excess thread, and add a dab of Super Glue to secure the knots and the end caps in place. **G**

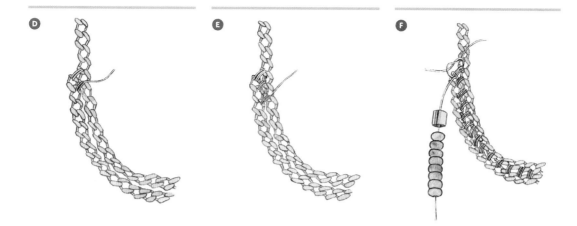

Attach the braid

10 Cut 5 skeins of the embroidery thread into 1 yd/1 m sections. Reserve 3 yd/3 m of embroidery thread.

11 Use half of the reserved thread to wrap around the bundle of thread created in step 5 about 1 in/2.5 cm from the ends. Knot it, trim any excess thread, and add a dab of Super Glue to secure the knot. Divide the knotted thread into the three sections and braid them until you have about 17 in/43 cm of braid. Leave the end loose for now. If you'd like, use a binder clip to hold it in place for extra security while you work, but the thread tends to hold its shape well.

12 To attach the braid, lay the necklace on the work surface so that it maintains its curved shape. Position the braid inside the curve and shape it into place so that it creates a complementary curve. With the thread doubled, thread the needle with the last long strand of embroidery thread. Use it to stitch the braid to the chain. To do so, sew the needle through several of the closest threads and tie this to the first link on the longest chain. Add a dab of Super Glue to secure the knot. **H**

continued

Once you've mastered lashing chain together, play with the elements that you attach to the chain. Rope or crystal chain are both lovely additions to a statement necklace or bracelet.

TIP

13 Lash each link of chain to the braid, picking up several threads with each stitch. As you reach the end of the braid, you may need to braid several more inches of thread in order to reach the end of the chain. Wrap the thread bundle, knot it, trim any excess thread, and add some Super Glue to secure the knot. **ⓘ**

Attach the crystals and clasp

14 Slide a headpin through each of the holes in the large crystal baguettes. Attach the crystal baguettes to the bottom of the necklace with a simple wrapped loop. Glue the metal setting on the top of each of the three black diamond baguettes to the metal setting on the bottom of the three center crystal baguettes with E-6000 glue.

15 Attach the large spring ring clasp to one side of the chain with two pairs of medium jump rings. Attach a large jump ring to the right-hand side of the chain with three pairs of medium jump rings. Since the necklace ends up being rather heavy, doubling up on the jump rings gives it more security.

SOURCES AND RESOURCES

JEWELRY FINDINGS AND COMPONENTS

Get to know the people at your local bead or jewelry shop, because they can be helpful resources when you're deciding which supplies you'll need for a project. This list is a mix of our local favorites and online resources for shopping from home.

Dreamtime Creations
This online destination has a range of rhinestones and crystals to add sparkle to your project.
www.dreamtimecreations.com

Fire Mountain Gems and Beads
This online shop is home to an overwhelming assortment of beads and findings in tons of plating options. They offer discounted pricing when you're stocking up on supplies.
www.firemountaingems.com

Metalliferous
This site is our go-to source for brass stampings, machined parts, wire, rod, and most things metal.
www.metalliferous.com

Ohio Beads
This online shop offers a large variety of harder-to-find chains and findings in an assortment of plating colors and finishes.
www.ohiobeads.com

Ornamentea
This North Carolina favorite was the first place we ever shopped for jewelry supplies. Their online shop has a wonderful selection of findings and filigree components.
www.ornamentea.com

Rio Grande
Rio is the place to go for sterling silver and gold metal components as well as semiprecious stones.
www.riogrande.com

Shipwreck Beads
Shipwreck has a huge selection of bead strands, findings, and components with competitive prices.
www.shipwreckbeads.com

Toho Shoji
Toho is the place to go for chic components and hard-to-find chains in any plating.
www.tohoshoji-ny.com

Wonder Sources
If you're looking for really special semiprecious stones, this is the spot. You'll find agate, pyrite, and amethyst sourced from all over the world.
www.wondersources.com

CRAFT AND SEWING MATERIALS

These are our go-to spots for everyday essentials like paint, ribbon, and fabric.

B&J Fabrics
This fabric mecca stocks hard-to-find fabric, including printed chiffon, lace, and poplin.
www.bandjfabrics.com

Dick Blick
From paint to polymer clay supplies, this is our one-stop shop. We especially love their professional-quality spray paint for quick color fixes.
www.dickblick.com

Pacific Trimming
We shop this trim store for its amazing selection of buttons, studs, and metal trimmings.
www.pacifictrimming.com

Purl SoHo
While Purl is known as a knitting store, we often stop by for a dose of inspiration, sewing supplies, and fabric.
www.purlsoho.com

Studs and Spikes
The name says it all. This online shop is the place to go for studs and spikes in any size or shape.
www.studsandspikes.com

VINTAGE RESOURCES

The listed vintage shops and shows carry much more than jewelry and supplies. They provide visual inspiration for designing your own projects.

Brimfield Antique Show
This small New England town in the United States turns into an enormous antique show for one week every May, June, and September.
www.brimfieldshow.com

eBay
We love eBay for everything from clip-on earrings to vintage crystal jewelry. With the right keyword search, you can find vintage pieces for a steal. Make sure to set up watch lists for future projects.
www.ebay.com

Etsy
In addition to vintage jewelry, Etsy has a selection of vintage beads and findings that are worth checking out, especially if you're looking for just a few of something.
www.etsy.com

Pippin Vintage Jewelry
This tiny jewel box of a shop is home to an ever-changing assortment of affordable vintage custom jewelry and jewelry parts that are perfect for turning into statement jewelry.
www.pippinvintage.com

Rose Bowl Flea Market
This is arguably the best flea market in California. It's held the second Sunday of every month, rain or shine, all year round.
www.rgcshows.com/rosebowl.aspx

Tinsel Trading Company
This New York shop and online store stocks fancy vintage trims, tassels, and ephemera.
www.tinseltrading.com

SUGGESTED READING

These books and online destinations top our list of references for technical information and inspiration.

Online sites

Garance Doré

Her infectious take on fashion and life is a daily read in our studio. Her blog includes illustrations, video, and hilarious commentary on the fashion world at large.
www.garancedore.fr/en

Style.com

The bible of runway fashion, this website has an encyclopedic collection of images from practically every runway show. Use the details tab available on popular shows for high-res images of the jewelry from the show.
www.style.com

Tommy Ton

This street photographer captures the best off-the-catwalk looks. We use his site to check out his close-up shots of accessories real girls are wearing and how they're styling it.
www.jakandjil.com

Books and catalogs

The Complete Metalsmith: An Illustrated Handbook

by Tim McCreight
This comprehensive guide to metalsmithing has easy-to-follow illustrations for beginners and can be used as a complete reference for more experienced makers.

Fashion Jewelry: The Collection of Barbara Berger

by Harrice Simons Miller
This book accompanied the exhibition of the same name at the Museum of Art and Design in New York City. It contains images of extravagant fashion and costume jewelry pieces that celebrate craftsmanship as well as creativity.

Jewelry: From Antiquity to the Present

by Clare Phillips
This survey of jewelry from the Western world often inspires us to use new-to-us silhouettes and techniques. Phillips highlights both craftsman-made jewelry and designer pieces.

Jewels by JAR

by Adrian Sassoon
JAR, or Joel Arthur Rosenthal, is the eccentric Willy Wonka of the jewelry world. His stunning pieces are some of the most sought after in the world.

The Theory and Practice of Goldsmithing

by Erhard Brepohl and Tim McCreight
We purchased this book on our first day at New York's Fashion Institute of Technology. Its technical explanations and diagrams are often helpful for problem solving.

The **auction catalogs** from fine jewelry auctions can be found online as well as at used bookstores or eBay for as little as a few dollars. Sotheby's Magnificent Jewels and Important Jewels auctions are the ones to look for when you're browsing or if you've ever wondered what a 50-karat pink diamond looks like.
www.christies.com and www.sothebys.com

ACKNOWLEDGMENTS

Our gratitude goes to:

Our amazing team, who rise to the occasion every day: Rachel Heaton, Mari Sheibley, Pooja Chakraborty, Evie Shaffer, and Tate Obayashi.

Casey Driskill and Leah Pierce for their help, friendship, and modeling skills.

This book would not have been possible without the support and guidance of our editor Lisa Tauber and the team at Chronicle Books.

Janet would like to thank:
Collin, for his unconditional love and support. My mom and dad, who taught me how to live creatively and without fear of failure.

Katie would like to thank:
Mary, Joseph, and Samuel.

INDEX